DREAMS

and

Nightmares

St. Luke's C.E. Primary School

THIS BOOK IS A PUBLICATION OF
McQueen Publishing
4 Johnson Close
Lancaster
LA1 5EU

Copyright © 2014
by McQueen Publishing
All Rights Reserved

First Edition July 2014

This book is protected by copyright.
No part of it may be reproduced, stored in a retrieval system or
transmitted in any form or by any means, electronic or otherwise,
without written permission from the copyright owners.

ISBN 978 0 9573374 9 7

Printed by
Berforts Information Press
in the UK

This book was written by
and belongs to:

I am a published author. I
am proud to be one of the
writers of this book.

My contribution can
be found on page(s):

I am [ ] years old.

The Author

This is a photo of me at time of writing.

Foreword

'Follow your dream...take one step at a time and don't settle for less, just continue to climb. Follow your dream... If you stumble, don't stop and lose sight of your goal, press on to the top...For only on top can we see the whole view, can we see what we've done and what we can do, can we then have the vision to seek something new...

Press on, and follow your dream.'

Amanda Bradley

I am very excited to bring you our first ever published book and we hope you enjoy it. It is a varied collection of writing by the children of Skerton St Luke's CE VA School which certainly reflect the book's title 'Dreams and Nightmares'.

It is very true that the best ideas are living inside you. An author's challenge is to dig them out and tell the story only they can tell. That is, I hope what every child has done in this book.

A huge thanks to the staff of Skerton St Luke's who provided lots of stimulus and support to help our young writers become published authors. Let's hope this is just the beginning. Keep writing!

Mrs Catherine Armistead
Head Teacher 2014

Reception

The Enchanted Wood

Once upon a time the Gingerbread Man went up the beanstalk to the giant's house. The giant wanted to eat the Gingerbread Man. The dragon saved him. The Gingerbread Man got home safely and lived happily ever after.

By: Jaden Gourlay

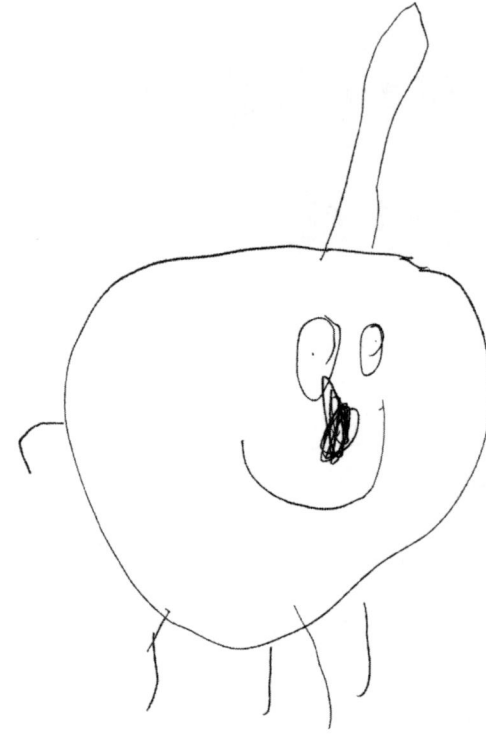

Once upon a time in the woods there was a unicorn and a bird. They lived in a magic wigwam. The magic wigwam landed on the ice lake. The bird and the unicorn picked it up and put it on dry land. They loved dry land because it was warm and nice. They lived there happily ever after.

By: Isabelle Whiteside

Once upon a time Tinkerbell was flying around the forest. The wolf chased her. She flew up the beanstalk and flew into the giant's castle. Tinkerbell chopped the beanstalk down. The little wolf came back to the forest and Tinkerbell lived happily ever after.

By:
Dexter Mulholland-Helme-Kelsall

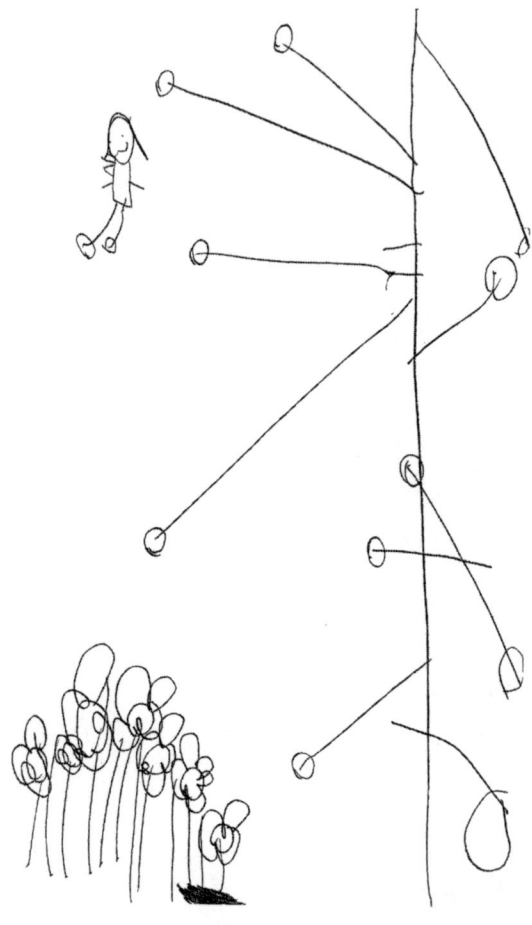

Once upon a time a nice fairy flew up to get some apples off the tree for her friend. The dragon stole the apples. He burnt people when they tried to get the apples. The unicorn killed the dragon. The fairy went to the unicorn's house and lived happily ever after.

By: Annabelle Hunt

Once upon a time the Gingerbread Man went to the house. He jumped on the fox and the cow wanted to eat him. The fox ran away fast. A dog rescued the Gingerbread Man and helped him find some food.

By: Shane Bradshaw

Once upon a time a princess was picking flowers by the dragon's cave. The dragon wanted to eat the princess. The prince climbed up the beanstalk and rescued the princess. The prince and the princess went back to their castle.

By: Nathan Taylor

Once upon a time a pretty pink fairy was getting some pixie dust from the hollow tree. The other fairies had taken it to the castle. The Queen Fairy magicked some more. She got some fairy dust from the hollow tree and could fly again.

By: Maggie Strachan

Once upon a time Jack wanted to find somebody spooky. He climbed down a dark tree in a spooky wood. He found a spooky boy and Jack was scared. Then they made friends and they played in the castle. They went to the little boy's house to play. They had fun and lived happily ever after.

By: Leo Robson

Once upon a time a good dragon was blowing fire in the dark, scary woods. The wicked queen took his fire away. The dragon flew to her castle and snatched it back. The dragon went back to his cave in the forest. They lived happily ever after.

By: Harry Shuttleworth

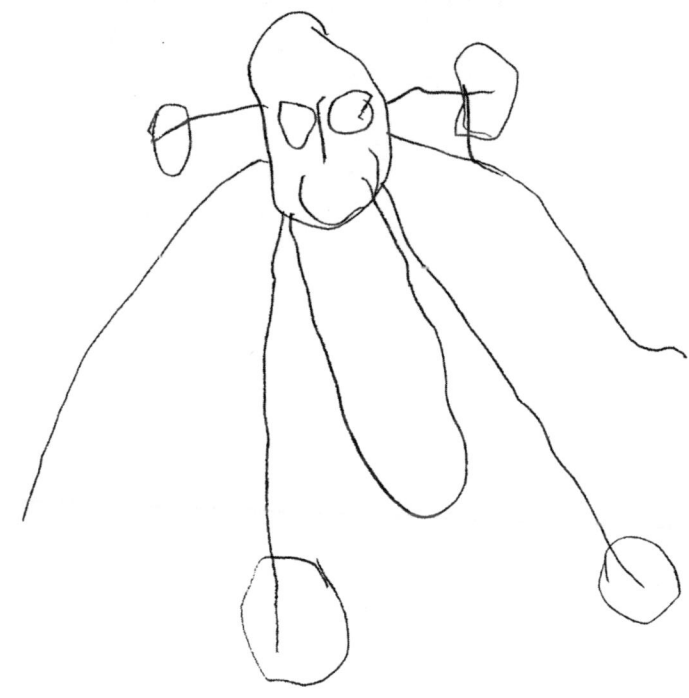

Once upon a time Cinderella was looking for her friends. She went to the magical wood and saw her favourite animals. She wasn't nice with the animals. Then the animals ran away from her. She made friends and they didn't run away. Cinderella played catch with the animals in the magic wood. They lived happily ever after.

By: Daisy Brown

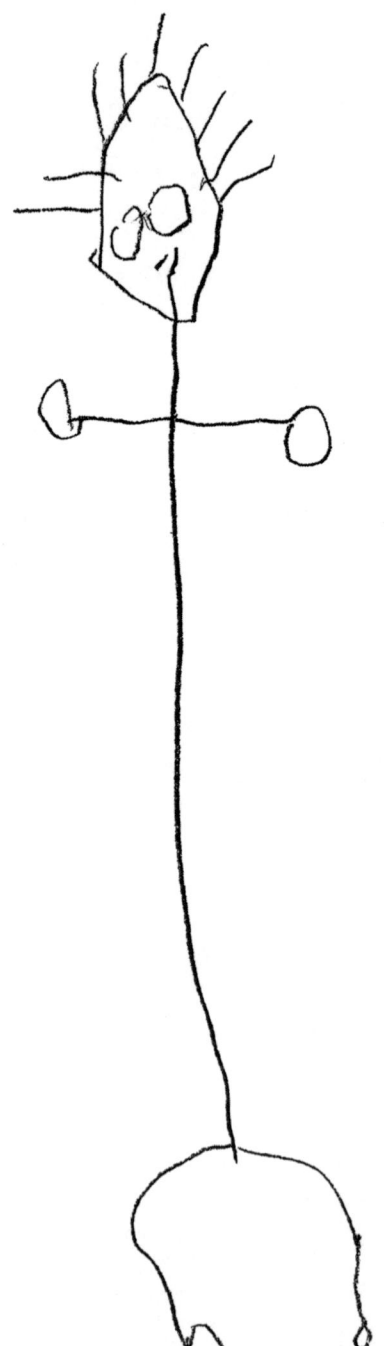

Once upon a time the prince was digging for diamonds in the mine. The witch did some magic on the prince. The tree did a spell to help him. The tree broke her wand and the prince went back to the mine.

By: Thomas Smith

Once upon a time a witch wanted to make magic. She walked to her spooky house. She wanted to do a spell to make a boy but it didn't work. Then she did it again and it worked. They went to her spooky house and made magic spells. They held hands and lived happily ever after.

By: George
    Gardner

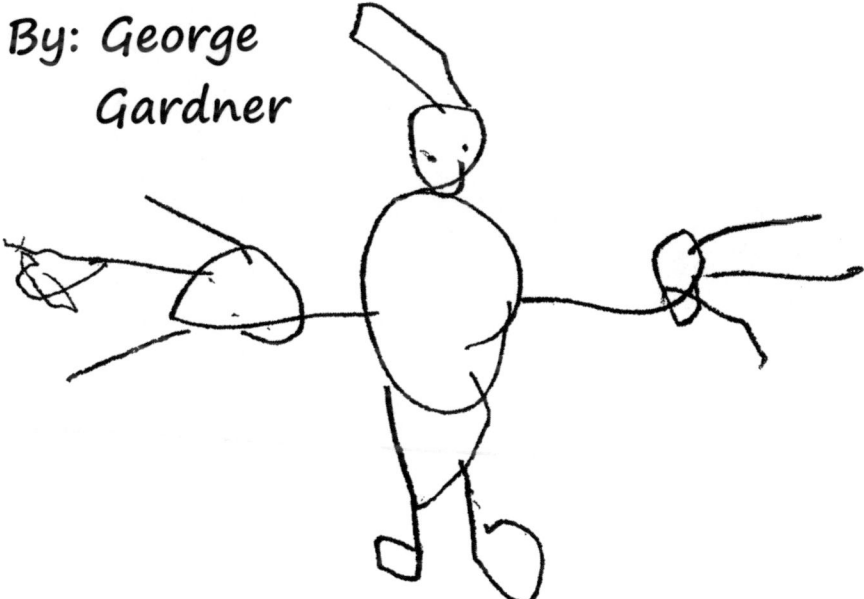

Once upon a time the Hulk was looking for a bad man in a sparkly, shiny wood. The bad man kicked him. The Hulk kicked the bad man up into a tree. The Hulk threw him down from the tree. The bad man ran away.

By: Alfie Lynch

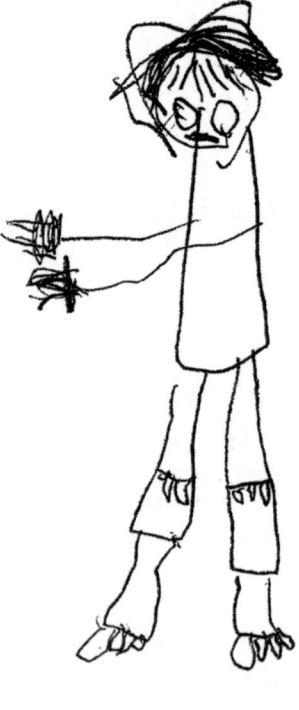

Once upon a time Snow White had gone to sleep in the forest. When she woke up she found a giant. The dragon chased the giant away. Snow White went back to her castle and she lived happily ever after.

By: Amelia Vallente

Once upon a time the Gingerbread Man was having a picnic in the meadow. A wizard took the Gingerbread Man to his castle. Some sand made a big path for him to get out. He ran down the path. He found his picnic and started eating it all over again.

By: Henry
     Newby

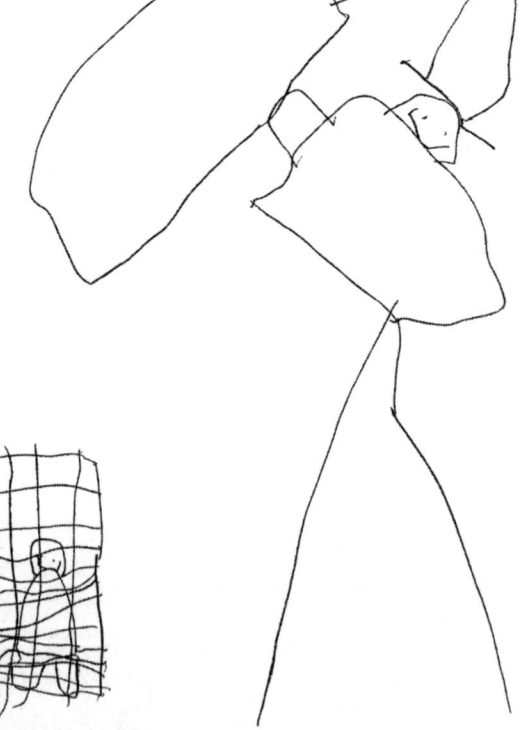

Once upon a time Snow White went to see the dwarves. She knocked on the door. Her dress was in the three bear's house. The three bears climbed up the potato tree and gave it back. Snow White married the prince and they lived happily ever after.

By: Phoebe O'Keeffe

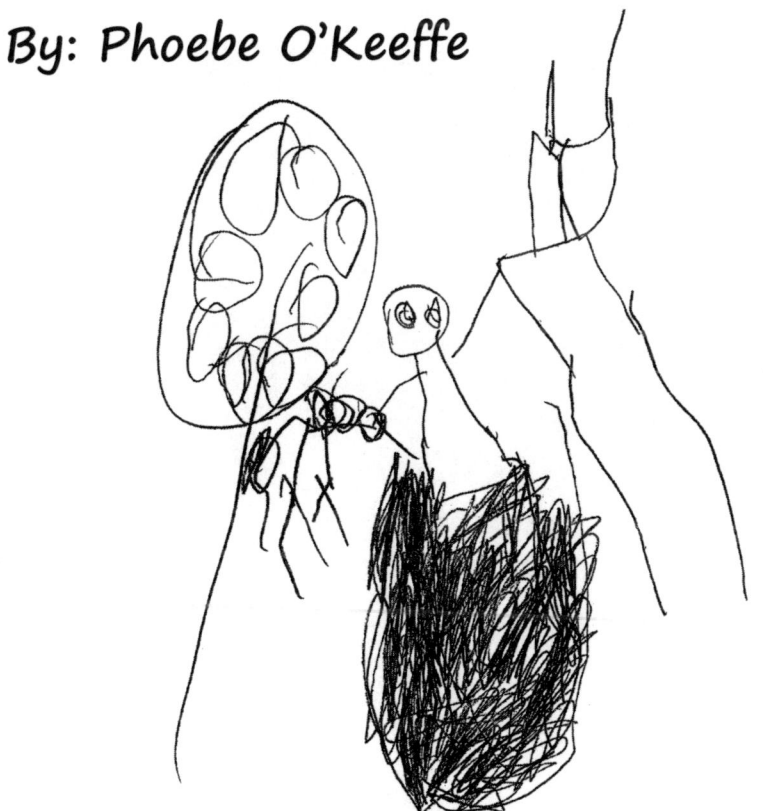

Once upon a time there was an angry giant in the castle. He was having his breakfast. The Twinkle Trees were too bright. The dragon turned them down. He put the Twinkle Trees in the bin and lived happily ever after.

By: Summer Clayworth-Jury

Once upon a time the good witch was flying and jumping over trees in the scary forest. The bad witch wanted to get the good witch. The good giant saved the good witch. The good witch and the good giant went to see the giant's family.

By: Charlie Lomax

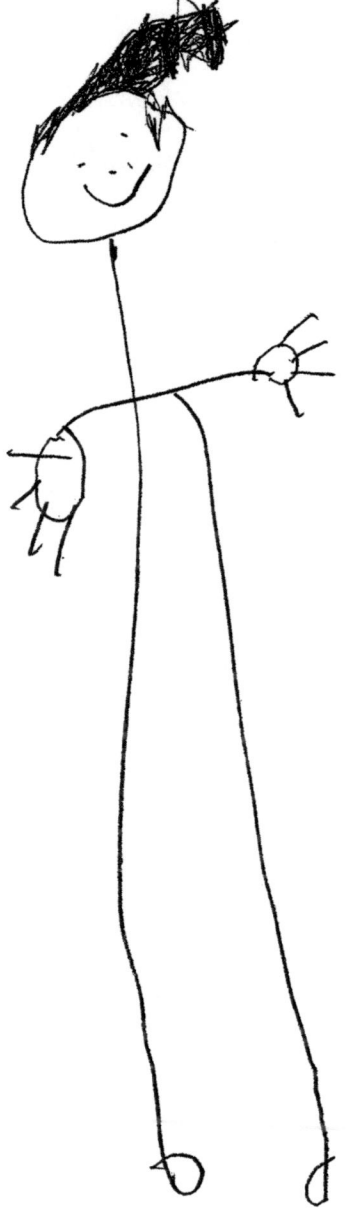

Once upon a time Lizard Man was walking in the forest looking for stones. He tripped over a rock. He asked the giant to smash the rock and help him. Lizard Man and the giant threw stones in the river. They lived happily ever after.

By: Vinnie Parkin

Once upon a time a pretty fairy was picking flowers for the King.

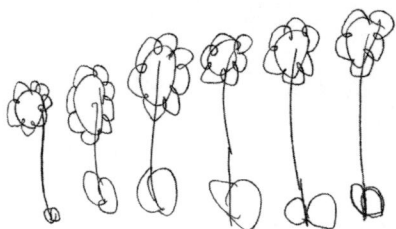

The wicked Queen took the flowers away. The King told her to put them back in the forest.

The fairy gave the flowers to the King. The fairy lived happily ever after.

By: Ella Gardner

Once upon a time in a spooky forest a dragon was trying to get the naughty door to go away. The naughty door ate the dragon. Then the dragon breathed fire on the door and then the door spat him out. The dragon

went to a magic forest. When he was at the forest he met some fairies and lived happily ever after. **By: Liam Bateson**

22

Once upon a time Snow White was in the castle. She was hiding from a big ogre. She hid under the bed. The ogre didn't find Snow White and she lived happily ever after.

By: Lexie Clements

Once upon a time a dwarf was in his house making a cup of tea. A dragon came and breathed fire. The dwarf threw the cup of tea and the fire went out. The dragon ran away because he hated tea. The dwarf lived happily ever after.

By: Leo Donnelly

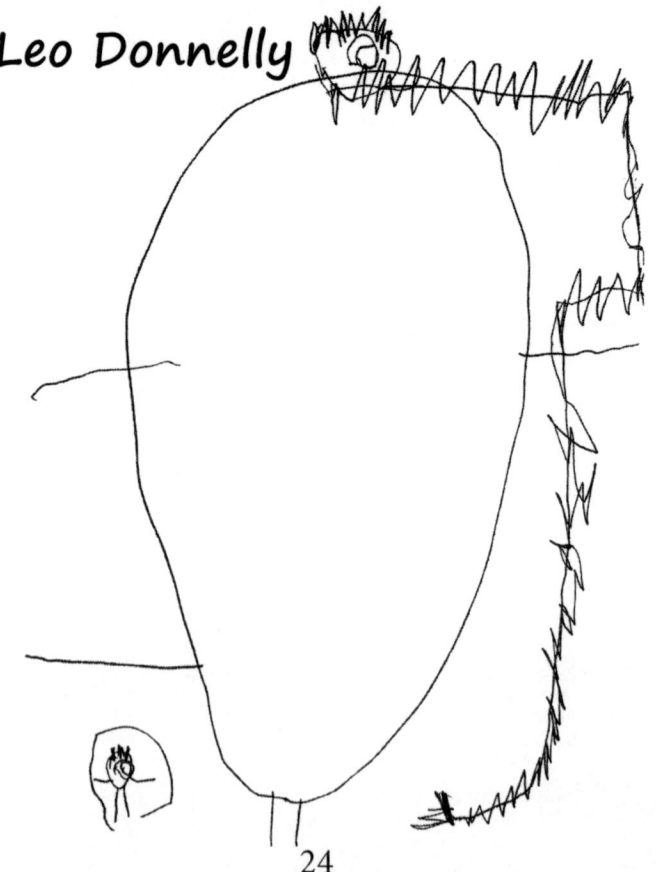

Once upon a time a unicorn was waiting for her friends on the grass in the fairy forest. She couldn't find her friends. The wizard sang a magic song and her friends came to her. They played hide and seek in the unicorn's garden. The friends all lived happily ever after.

By: Rhianna Duncan

Once upon a time Rapunzel was getting dressed upstairs in the castle. She couldn't find her dress. A magic bear found it. She went to a ball and met a prince. They lived happily ever after.

By: Robert
    Brooks

Once upon a time a prince w e n t through a scary wood. He wanted to find the princess in a castle. The giant tried to kill the princess and eat her. The prince killed the giant. They went to the palace and lived happily ever after.

By: Angel Grenfell

Once upon a time Snow White was dancing on a slippy black tree. She fell off and hurt herself. The dwarf put a plaster on and made it better. The dwarf hugged her and they lived happily ever after.

By: Callum Benson

Once upon a time Louie dressed up as a dragon and he went to the treasure tree. There was no treasure in the tree. A witch came and made the treasure come back. They took the treasure home to make some gold. They were very rich and lived happily ever after.

By: Louie Brown

Once upon a time there were some happy talking trees in a sunny forest. It was too bright and the leaves died. The fairy made a spell to make it spring time sooner. The talking trees played catch in the forest.

By: Phoebe Atkin

Once upon a time the wicked witch flew over the scary woods. She wanted to go to Snow White's palace. The wicked witch turned Snow White into a baddie. A fairy came and turned her back into a goodie. Snow White got the wand and turned the witch into a frog.

By: Ben Naylor

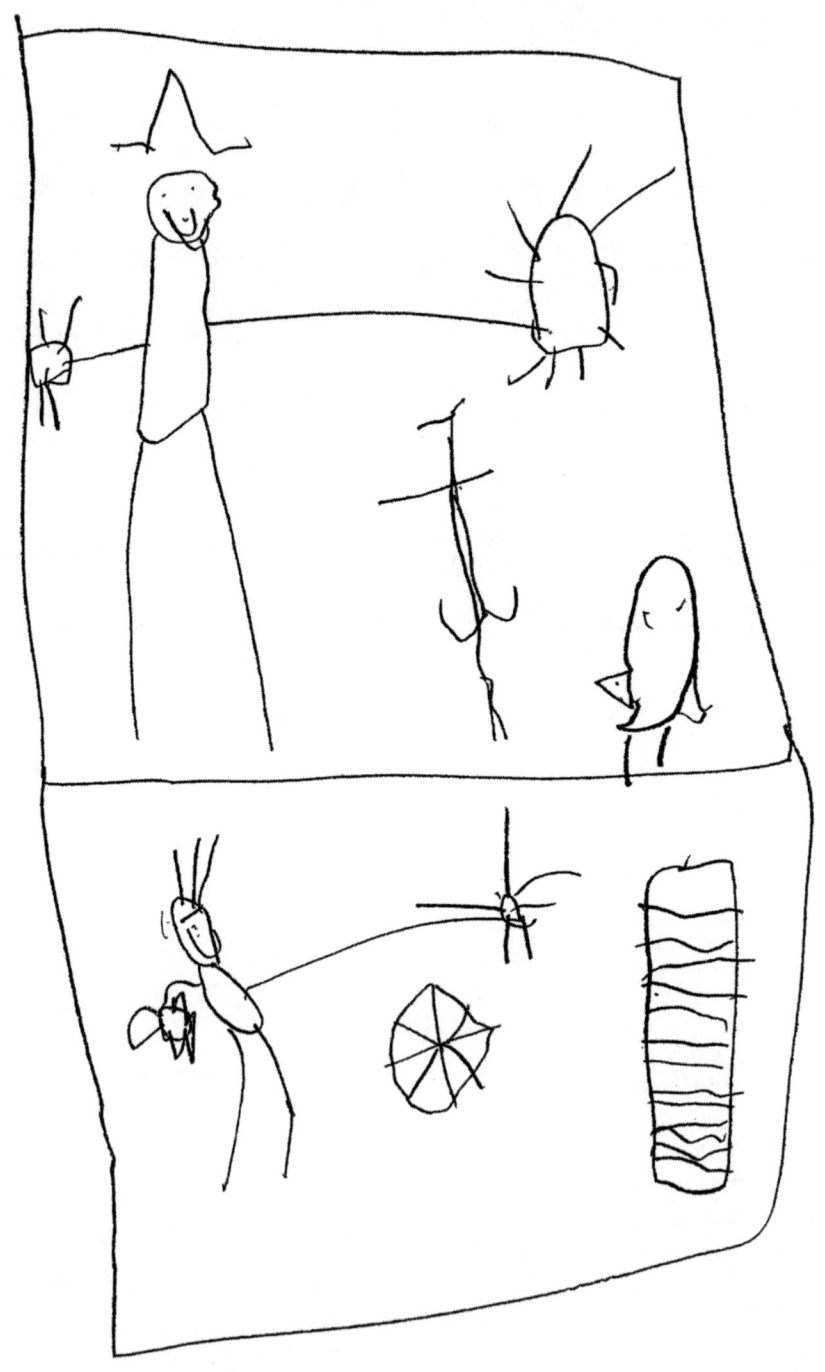

Year 1

Last Night I Dreamt I was a Pirate!

Last night I dreamt I was a pirate... Firstly, the fat pirate jumped onto the pink boat and sang a pirate song. After that the fat pirate made me walk the plank. The fat pirate was kind and shared treasure. I saw X marks the spot. Then the pirate chopped my arm off and I started a sword fight. After that I got on the pirate ship and I picked up a spade and dug a hole. Lastly, I spent my money on toys.

By: Bethany Coates

Last

night I dreamt I was a pirate... I was digging up the treasure chests and I took them both to my pirate ship. My crew were proud of me. But just as we thought we were rich six other pirates came and took both of our chests.

The six mean pirates were grumpy and cruel. They wouldn't give the treasure back so we fought them instead.

They nearly won but we won instead and we cut their feet and eyes off. We got the treasure back from the mean pirates.

By: Eleanor Dowler

Last night I dreamt I was a pirate...

It was scary! First, I went out to sea on my brown, big boat. Next, I saw X marks the spot and dug a deep hole. I dug a deep hole and I found treasure and there was gold coins.

After that I sailed back and spent it all on toys. I played with them and it was fun.

By: James Kerr

Last night I dreamt I was a pirate... First I had a sword fight and we went to find treasure.

A pirate tried to chop off my legs. Next we jumped on the pink ship. It had a skull and crossbones and lots of flags. Lastly, we found the treasure and we had diamonds and money.

By: Ellie-Jo Carradice

Last
night I dreamt I was a pirate... I had a sword fight with a fat pirate. I won the map from the fat pirate. I got the map and there was a compass...

...with the treasure. Next, I walked into a trap. I got my sword and I set myself free. Then I found the treasure. It had gold inside.

By: Kyle Robinson

Last
night I dreamt I was a pirate... I jumped on my ship and had a sword fight. I made someone walk the plank. He fell in the water. I found the treasure chest. It was in the wreck. There was lots of diamonds.

By: Harry Percival

Last night I dreamt I was a pirate... and I had a sword fight. I was the captain. I made my crew scrub the decks. Pirate Bogey Nose got my sword he put the sword on the bridge. He jumped on the Pirate Island. He managed to get the treasure. He got attacked by other pirates. I grabbed the treasure.

By: Mollie-May Green

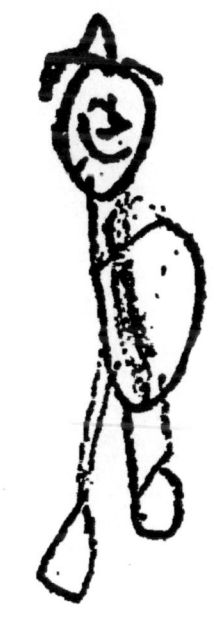

Last night I dreamt I was a pirate... I saw a pirate and he was very nasty and didn't have manners. Then he got his sword out and had a sword fight. Then I went on my pirate ship. I went to the island and stole the treasure. It was loads of shiny gold dubloons.

By: Charlie Horrocks

Last night I dreamt I was a pirate... I was on a ship. Next, I was sailing for treasure with my crew and we ended having a sword fight with a stupid pirate. I stole treasure from another pirate ship. I battled another pirate ship and I won the battle. I shot the cannon. I got the treasure from the secret base and they stole it back. I went on another adventure and sailed for more treasure.

By: Daniel Corless

Last night I dreamt I was a pirate... First, we sailed on an orange ship and we looked on our treasure map. We were near to the treasure and we were going to fight. We won. Lastly, we found the treasure.

By: Gianluca Gardiner

Last night I dreamt I was a pirate...

I was the captain of a pirate ship and my ship colour is brown and yellow. I was singing a pirate song.

I was cleaning the boat. Next, I had a swim in the sea. I climbed the rigging. After I looked for treasure and I dug in the sand.

Then I got the treasure. Then I ran to my pirate ship with the treasure.

By: Ted Stoney

Last night I dreamt I was a pirate... I had a sword fight with the pirates. I put my coat on. I went to get the treasure. It was on an island. It was lots of sweets.

By: Ben Atkinson

Last night I dreamt I was a pirate... I dug for treasure. I tried to lift the treasure. I finally got it.

By: Leon Bartholomew

Last night I dreamt I was a pirate... I jumped on a pirate ship and sang a song. I swung on the rope. I found the treasure.

By: Liam Fall

Last night I dreamt I was a pirate... I am captain Ellie and I boss people around. Next, someone got on our ship and stole our chest. Then I fought a pirate called Sam. He was stupid and crazy. The pirate said, 'Arrrrrrrrrrrrrrrrrrr.'

'Shut up', I said.

Then I went to the island to get lots of gold dubloons in a chest. Lastly, I made someone walk the plank. 'Jump!'

By: Ellie Robson

Last night I dreamt I was a pirate... First we had a sword fight with the other pirates. We won and we got the treasure map and we got the chest. I made the bad pirate walk the plank and a shark came and got him.

By: Poppy Beswick

Last

night I dreamt I was a pirate... First I fired the cannons they made a noise. I got the treasure from the secret base. I took it to my pirate ship. I counted sixteen diamonds and one coin. I felt happy.

By: Charlie Davis

Last

night I dreamt I was a pirate... The large pirate kidnapped someone. His boat was large and the boat was massive. The skull was black and the pirate wore a red jacket and black trousers and the bad sharks attacked when the pirate tried to get the treasure.

By: Lauren Satterley

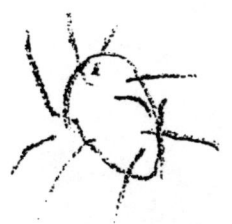

Last night I dreamt I was a pirate... I had a sword fight. It was scary and the pirate cut my leg off. Then I got the treasure chest over to the ship.

By: Becky Turner

Year 1 - I Dreamt I was a Pirate!

Last night I dreamt I was a pirate...Then I had a sword fight with a hairy pirate. I found treasure on a desert island and I found a map in a tree. I got it with a long stick. I shared the money all out. I saved some for me.

By: Evie Lamb

Last night I dreamt I was a pirate... I had a sword fight with Captain Hook. I found treasure. I found a chest on the beach and inside it was a sparkly crown. I went on the ship and I went home.

By: Ella Norris

Last night I dreamt I was a pirate... I jumped onto the pirate ship. I fought a pirate. He cut my leg off. I found the treasure. I was happy.

By: Charlie Michie

Last night I dreamt I was a pirate... I went to sea on my ship. My ship is gigantic. I looked for treasure. I found it on an island. I was happy.

By: Jessica Tassart

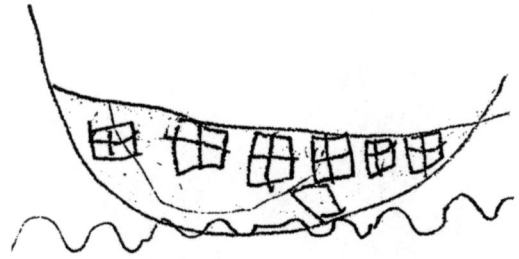

Last night I dreamt I was a pirate... Firstly, I saw something glow in the dark. I went through a keyhole and I brought the chest. Pirates tried to steal treasure off me. I chopped the mates head off. I got some more treasure.

By: James Capper

Last night I dreamt I was a pirate... Firstly, I hunted for treasure. Next I dug for treasure. It was easy. Inside it was gold treasure. I took it home. I bought a gold hola hoop!

By: Bonnie Clarke

Last night I dreamt I was a pirate... Firstly, I found an island but other pirates took the treasure. I attacked their ship. I won. I got the treasure. I made a fortune! It was fun.

By: Matthew Bates

Last night I dreamt I was a pirate... With my crew we went on the huge pirate ship. We were far away from treasure and we were singing. We got the treasure. Inside the treasure box was sweets.

By: Jessica Turner

Last night I dreamt I was a pirate... I had a sword fight with Pirate Bogey Nose. I found a treasure chest. It was full of gold. I was happy.

By: Mickey Moreira

Last night I dreamt I was a pirate... I made someone walk the plank and then he fell into the water. He went on a dolphin and came back on to the ship and then he fired a cannon. He gave me the treasure map. I said, 'Thank you.'

I went on the island and found the treasure. We got back on the ship and we sailed home.

By: Teagan Hebblethwaite

Last night I dreamt I was a pirate... It was a stormy night. In the morning me and my crew sailed off looking for treasure. But we crashed into a ginormous island. On the island we found some treasure. I shared it.

By: Evelyn Leong-Smith

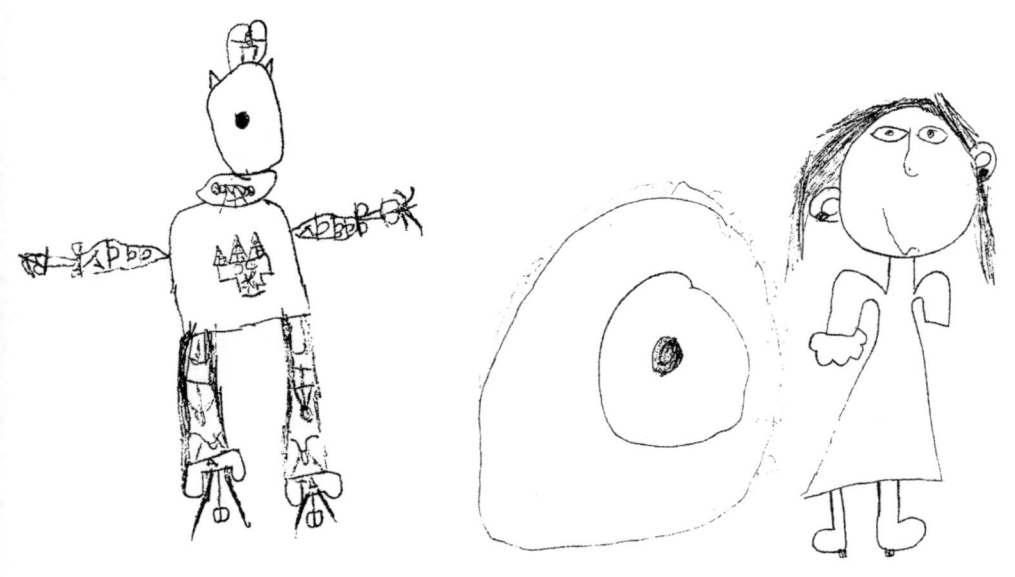

Year 2

Lauren Revie

I woke up and a portal appeared in my room. I went through it and I was in Candy Land. A girl was singing by a castle. 'What's your name?' I said.

'My name is Kiera,' she replied.

Suddenly a fairy appeared. 'Sweet Tooth is taking over the world. Help! We need you to save Candy Land. You will need to work together to find Elsa and to bring back more Candy, Oh no! Candy Cops!'

'Kiera, what are we going to do?'

'Follow me,' said Kiera. 'Here jump in this portal and this will all go away.'

I jumped in the portal sadly and said goodbye to Kiera and Candy Fairy.

'You can see us on your phone,' said the Candy Fairy.

It had been the best day of my life. I don't know what happened to Sweet Tooth.

Hollie Oldcorn

On the gloomiest night I dreamed I was in Rainbow Land. I woke up and I was in a magical place. I was extremely scared. I met a rainbow over the sea.

Suddenly, I heard a strange noise and I thought it sounded like a monster. It appeared to me. The monster was green, slimy and dripping. He nearly got me but my karate saved me because I thought about what I was going to do. I eventually got out of all the mess and I was happy.

At that moment the monster was alive. I could not believe my eyes. Suddenly, the rainbows saved my life and they turned out looking like a motorbike racer.

The monster was never seen again and the rainbow's said, 'Hooray! Hooray!'

We all had to go back to our own place and on the way home I got covered in green and red patches.

'Why are you covered in colours?' my mum asked.

But I could not tell her. It was my secret. It was my dream!

Hollie Oldcorn

Samuel Lomax

One dark stormy night Spiderman, Max and his friend Batman, woke up. A bright shiny portal suddenly appeared in their bedroom. Spiderman, Max and Batman jumped into it. Just at that moment they appeared in a haunted house! It was quite scary. It was dark and gloomy. Giant spiders crawled quickly up the walls.

Suddenly, they heard a loud trembling noise coming from the monster's bedroom. Spiderman, Max and his friend Batman, quickly jumped back into the portal. Finally, they were back home safe.

Oliver Nuttall

Once there was a boy called Oliver. He was asleep when suddenly he heard a noise. It woke him up. He went into a portal to a Land of Wands and Spells.

It looked amazing! He saw the wand he had always wanted. It was as big as a banana and as straight as a pencil.

Then he heard a noise. It was a witch. She was massive. Everyone ran into the shops to hide. They locked their doors but nothing could stop the witch. Oliver unlocked a door. He tried to use his wand, it didn't work. Who would stop her?

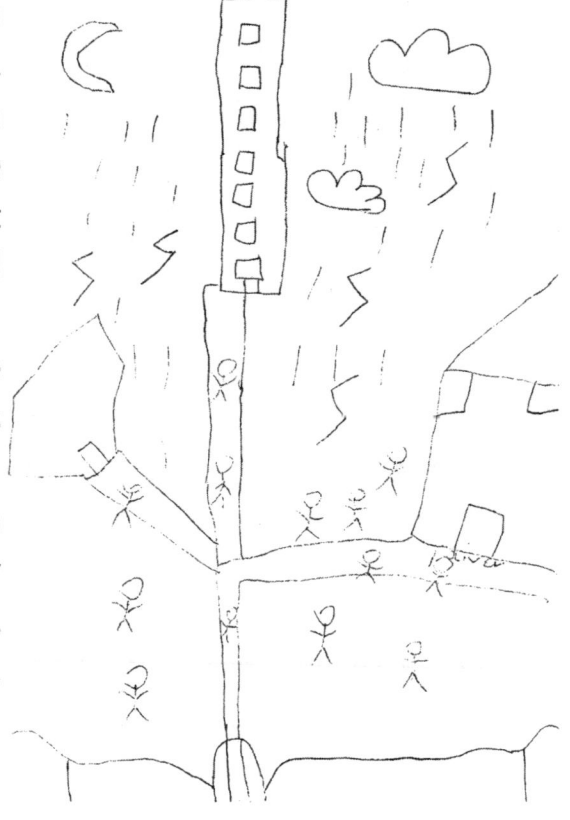

Oliver ran to the portal but it was gone!

Suddenly, a bunch of heroes came. They defeated the witch. Everyone cried, 'Wahoo!'

Tom Barton

One scary dark night a portal appeared. We jumped in, my Mum, Louie and I. We were stuck but we had bigger problems. A karate zombie locked us in a dungeon.

We were only given bread and water, it made us sad. I worried how we would ever get home.

Then Louie had an idea!

He used a super power he forgot he had and laser beamed the dungeon's door. Louie saved us. We ran really fast to the portal and flew through. I don't ever want to go back there again!

Jessica Lefever

A very long time ago a Land of Princesses was hidden through a magic door in Dalton Square, but nobody went through until...

The day when Jessica Lefever wanted to go to a place where no one had ever been. She dressed in her favourite party dress then she set off to find the Land of Princesses.

At last Jessica found the magic door, she opened it and flew through the portal into the land. As soon as she got there she turned into Sleeping Beauty, her dress became sparkly.

She named herself Aurora. She found a beautiful palace where she danced at a ball. Suddenly, she saw Belle. She asked to be sisters. 'Yes,' she said.

They happily danced together.

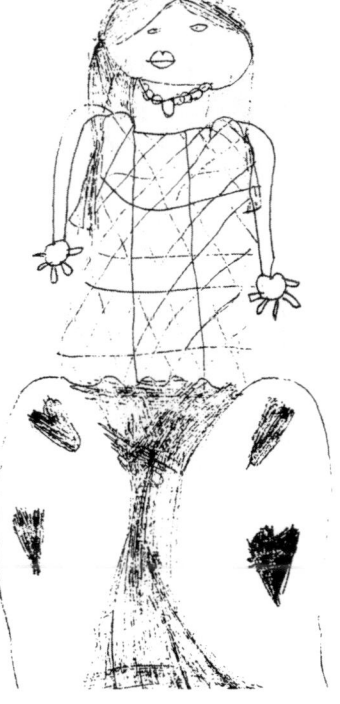

Suddenly, she had to go home. She was still a princess. She didn't tell anyone because it was her secret. She knew where the door was so she visited again and again and again and again until she was 81.

Thomas Seaton

Oliver, Sam and I were washing Samson. He is my dog. We heard a Hhhhhhmmming sound. It was a Nether Portal. We stood inside it.

We turned into Block Super Heroes. I was Torch, Oliver was Superman, Sam was Spiderman and Samson was Robin.

When we were in the Nether Portal we saw a super villain. He was going to explode the portal so we were trapped. He didn't want anyone else in the world to come through and see the future.

We attacked him to try and stop him. I threw a firebomb at him. Superman lasered his board. Spiderman kicked him in the face. Robin pecked him.

We heard a BOOM!

Supervillain turned into a huge monster. He threw us off the top of a building. But when we were falling we used our powers to trap him.

The portal was saved. But we couldn't find it to go home. It was lost. We were Block Super Heroes forever.

Jack Liptrot

On Thursday night Marlie and I woke up. We got out of bed and set off to Skeleton Land. Marlie and I saw skeletons, loads of skeletons in a dungeon.

We found a dinosaur skeleton. They were doing a chicken dance. We started to laugh. Just at that moment they saw us. They chased us and we ran as fast as a cheetah to get away!

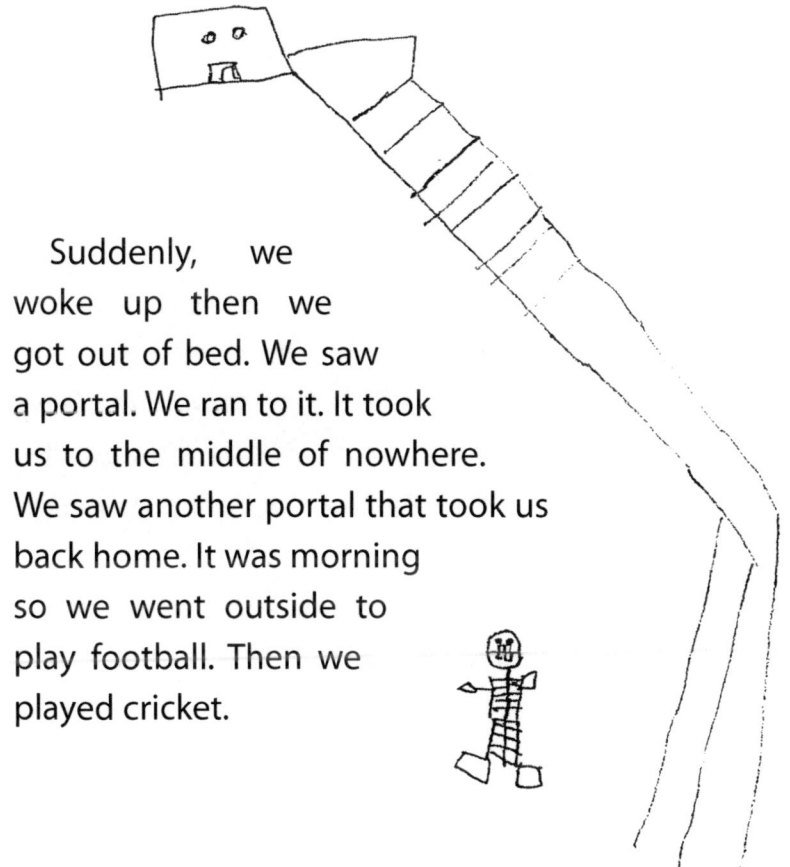

Suddenly, we woke up then we got out of bed. We saw a portal. We ran to it. It took us to the middle of nowhere. We saw another portal that took us back home. It was morning so we went outside to play football. Then we played cricket.

Daniel Wenlock

One dark night in my nightmare there was a haunted mansion. Suddenly, a spooky ghost appeared and made Gary jump. Everytime he saw the ghost Gary jumped.

Then he saw a tree with a finger moving. It had fruit on it. Gary knew if he ate the fruit he would die. Suddenly a door appeared so Gary went through it.

He found himself back in his bed. Then he woke up and he went downstairs. Just at that moment he saw his breakfast had been made. Who made it? Was it the spooky ghost?

Adam Holden

Am I in a dream or is it a nightmare? I am in the dark woods. Suddenly, a massive tree appeared. I climbed the dark tree. Just then, a man with a massive head scared me.

He didn't tell me his name. He pulled me up a ladder. Suddenly, I was in a wood. It was very spooky. Just then a man with dark armour, as dark as a bats cave and a massive eye appeared. He chased me into the castle. He was a knight from the olden days.

I hid in the cellar. I was petrified. He came into the same room as me.

A bucket fell over. Just then, he saw me. He captured me and took me to the main room. He locked me up.

Somehow a white rabbit tried to free me. But I couldn't get out. One day he snapped and hung me! I tremble in fear every night.

Chloe Hamilton

On my happy birthday night me and Mum went on an adventure to Flying Land where you can fly. Suddenly, a door appeared. Me and Mum went in the red door.

'Candy Land,' I said to Mum.

'Can we go to get some candy?' Mum shouted.

'Yes!'

Suddenly, my mum disappeared home. I was worried. I quickly sneaked some nice candy into my pocket. Somebody saw me. He had sharp boots. He was enormous! He was a giant.

He chased me through Flying Land. Suddenly, I disappeared. Finally, I got back home. My mum was in her bed asleep, snoring!

I never thought about it again but one day I thought about it. Just while I was walking to school. I saw the giant. The giant stared at me. He chased me. The giant caught me in his giant hands. I bit him and he dropped me. I landed on my feet and I ran back home. The giant was never to be seen again.

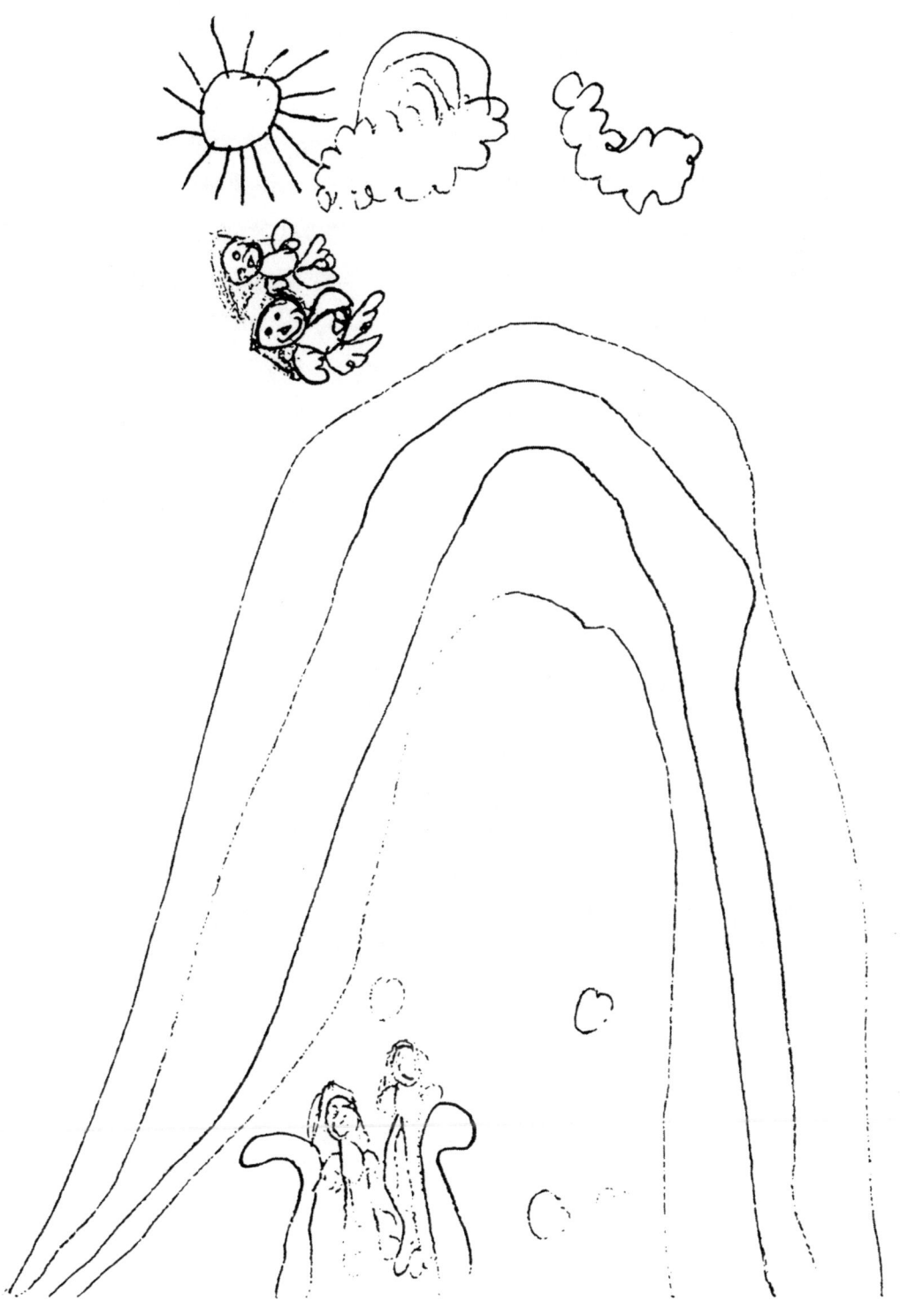

Leona Scholefield

It started at night. I was playing with my friends and suddenly a tarantula appeared in my hand. I was shocked! My friends had gone. I was scared. I thought that I was going away. Suddenly, I was in Spooky Land. 'Aaaaaaaarrrrrrrrgggggghhhhh!' I shouted.

I was scared so much it was more scary than a lion. A zombie cop put me in jail. I did not know what to do but the bats disappeared.

I was safe. Then I went home. But the tarantula was still there!

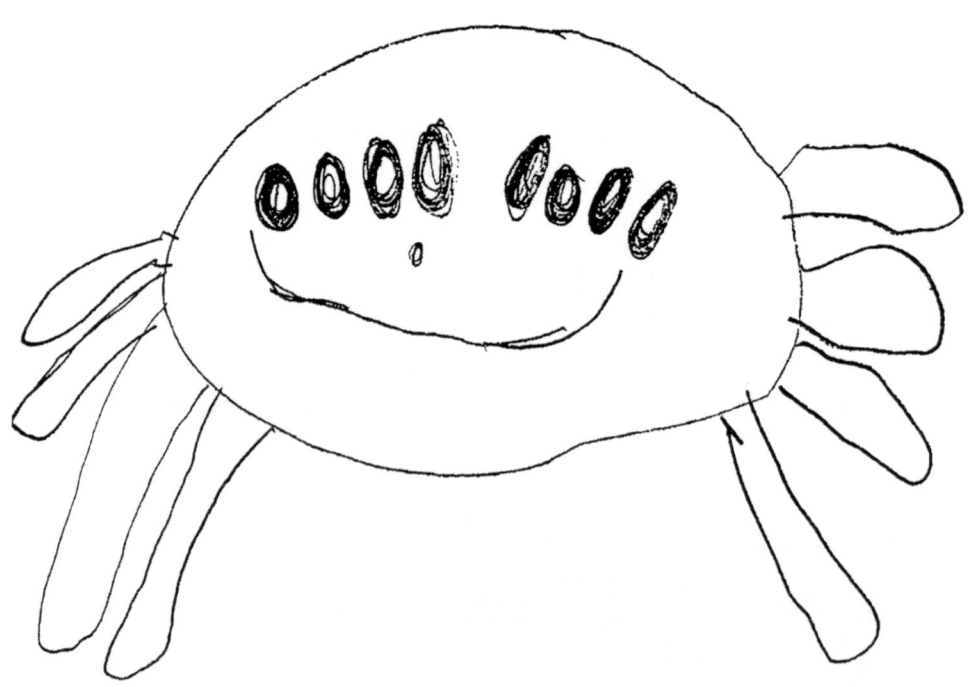

Zane Busby

One cold night in a village I was sleeping. I heard a crash from a window. It was a robbery. I got my gun and ran to the woods.

Indie my dog came too. Suddenly, we caught the robber. I shot him. I took him to hospital.

'Where have you been?' my mum said.

The next day I got scared. My mum was gone. I went to the woods again. She was there. She had turned into a vampire. I ran away really fast. I was safe.

Katie Stones

One cold night a girl was asleep She had a dream. A princess said, 'Who are you?'

'I am Katie,' she replied.

'Do you want to join us? 'Yes, come on,' said the princess.

The princess was scared. 'What's wrong?' she said.

'A witch is coming to attack me.'

'Don't worry.'

'Why, can you kill the witch?'

'Yes. I will need a sword.'

'I know where the swords are.'

'Really?'

'Yes.'

Then the witch came near her. The sword was straight.

The sword went through her body. Suddenly, the witch fell on the ground. They had a party. It was a good day.

Suddenly, she had to go. 'Goodbye. See you another day.'

This was the end of my dream.

Ruby Bateson

I t all started when I was in bed and I appeared in a strange land. I saw three people, Elsa, Anna and Hans. When I turned Elsa was gone. Suddenly, I turned to Hans and saw that he had gone too. When I turned to Anna she was gone!

Then Kristoff came walking by with Sven. They both looked at me. Sven thought I was a carrot so he licked me.

I asked Kristoff where I was. He said, 'We are in Frozen Land.'

I felt as cold as ice. I saw a slimy, icy, iky and gooey monster. I saw fire and ice blasters. I shot the fire blaster at the monster. I killed it.

I awoke and it was okay. It was only a dream!

Jack Lewis

One dark and gloomy night the stars appeared as sparkly as the Queen's crown. The stars were shining high in the sky. The footballers were playing football.

It was Liverpool versus Man City. Liverpool won 3 nil. They won the Champions League. It was amazing! The ball was a Nike ball.

Next they had another game. Liverpool versus Barcelona. Liverpool took the kick off. Suarez and Sterling scored 3 goals each. So Liverpool took the lead of 6 nil. But then Messi scored 2 goals and Dani Alves scored 1 goal. Then it was half time.

The game was back on. Barcelona took the kick off then Liverpool scored. Agger scored a header from a corner. Coutinho took the corner. My friend Jacob and I went to the great pitch Anfield. So it was 7 nil.

If this was true It would be my dream come true!

Brayden Rodgerson

On a snowy day I was outside building a snowman. I called him Olof. He loved warm hugs. We went ice skating. Eventually, my friends Elsa and Anna arrived but they disappeared suddenly.

I saw a monster. I got an axe. Elsa helped me. I whacked him and Elsa froze him. I hit him, he fell over and smashed into 10,000 pieces. Then Elsa disappeared again. I went through a door and suddenly I woke up. It was just a dream!

Ruby Bushell

Mum can I go into the woods on my own?

'Yes.'

'Thank you.'

Off I went. Suddenly, a ginormous bat came and nearly ate me. I was very frightened. I ran back home. It took ages.

Finally, it flew away so I tried again. I climbed the tree. Up in the clouds the land was Skeletons and Pony Land.

A skeleton and his pony came up to me and said, 'Can I live with you?'

'Yes. By the way, my name is Linza.'

'My pony is called Linza,' said the skeleton.

'Come on, climb down the ladder with me. Okay, this is the forest. Come into my house.' Off we went into the house. 'You are both going to sleep in my bedroom.'

The next day we went up the ladder to Rainbow land. We climbed the tree. We could take three rainbows. We all looked around. We couldn't find the ladder! Finally, we found the ladder.

Se we went down, displayed our rainbows then we went up the ladder to get one fancy rainbow. We went down the ladder and sold them all. We got £100.

The next day I told all of my friends about it. They were shocked. They wished they had come too.

Holly Cunningham

Once upon a time I went in the dark woods. I saw a pink tree. It was talking saying, 'Come to the Land of Birthdays.'

I climbed up the tree with my sister, Nicole and there was a cloud with a hole in it. I went through it. Nicole did too. We saw a Land of Birthdays.

I went to a shop and bought a chocolate cake. It was a big cake. Nicole bought seven candles. We bought some party rings. It was my birthday.

I blew out the candles it took me two times. I wished for a pink unicorn. My wish came true. I had a ride on the unicorn. Then we flew home. I opened my presents and I got a toy doll.

Holly Atkinson

My eyes were closed. I was asleep in my bed. I went to Dog Land. I brought two dogs home with me. My mummy let me keep them. I stroked and looked after my dogs.

Suddenly, I heard a Bang!

They started to bark. Suddenly, a monster tried to steel my dogs but I saved them.

The dogs barked as loud as they could.

The monster ran away, 'Aaaarrrrrrrgggggggghhhhh.'

We lived happily ever after.

Olivia Hunt

One cold dark winter's night a beautiful princess was going to pick some apples in the forest. Just at that moment she saw a rainbow and it had lots of different colours.

It lit up the sky, red like a tomato, pink like a pink bobble in my hair, yellow like a banana and as orange as the sun in the sky.

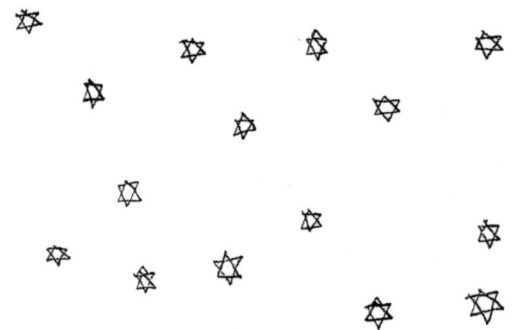

Suddenly, a large hairy, spotty monster jumped out from a tree! The princess screamed, 'Help! Help!' I helped her get home by saving her.

I put her in a box and took her home to her cosy cottage. Finally, I was in my bed.

Shirah Alexander

One sunny day I was going to play in the garden with my dog but when I went out of my door I was in a spooky land.

I saw my brother Dante there too. 'Where are we?' I asked him.

'In Monster and Shadow Land.'

'How do we get out Dante?'

'We have to go a long way. Lets go!'

We went through mountains, deserts and hills. When we got there we saw a dragon. It was sleeping. We tiptoed past the dragon. Dante hit the dragon by accident. The dragon was awake. Dante had a shield and a sword. Dante fought the dragon. Dante put his sword in the dragon. The dragon was dead.

We saw a door appear. We went through and we were back home. We had a picnic.

Lily Birkett

One sunny, bright, hot day I was having a picnic. After my food I was so bored. Just at that moment...What do you think it was?

I saw a dog. It was walking right up to me. It had legs, arms, a head and a body. It's a person. Oh wow it just turned into a tree! It stood right in front of me and turned back into a person. 'How do you do that? Magic!' I said.

'Ahhhhhh.'

'How can you talk magic? Okay, don't be freaky!'

'I'm not.'

'Just don't talk.'

Suddenly...

'I found a key,' I said.

'I found a door,' said freaky tree. 'Maybe the key will go in there then.'

They tried the key with the door and it worked. A rainbow appeared in front of them. 'It's a rainbow. Wow I could cry.'

'Go ahead and cry.'

'Let's get an ice cream. How much are ice creams? Nothing, wow that's amazing! Thank you.'

Me and freaky tree went on lots of rainbow rides. They were all free. Then it was twelve o'clock. 'I have to go. I promised Mum I would come home at twelve o'clock.

But then she was gone. Earlier, she was home. She saw her tree house. She thought it was the freaky tree. She told her mum about everything. She didn't believe her but when she told her about the ice cream she remembered that she had left it in her pocket. She tried to show her but it had melted. The next day Mum went shopping so I went back to freaky tree. What do you think happened?

Amelie Pritchard

One spooky halloween night a little girl named Amelie was with her family trick or treating when suddenly, she fell in a hole into a spooky land.

Just then a spooky castle appeared in front of her. When she knocked on the door, the doors opened by themselves. She went inside the castle when suddenly, the doors slammed with a big BANG!

Suddenly, everything went pitch black. She was so scared that she was shaking with fear. When she stopped she found a lightswitch. She turned it on and she was in a room full of bats.

She was terrified. She saw the scariest thing in the world! King and Queen bats with a scary Princess Bat with really dark black hair.

She was terrified. She could not help but want to scream. But she couldn't because she didn't want to wake them. She really wanted to get out of the spooky castle! But she couldn't.

Before she could get nervous she spotted a low window. She climbed out with the treasure that she found and ran home and they were rich. They lived happily ever after.

Amelie Pritchard

81

Annabel Johnson

Once I woke up it was still dark but I got up anyway. When I opened my door a portal appeared. I was lost for words. I went through it. Then I saw people and shops and everyone was happy. Even the animals were happy. I was amazed.

Just then a fairy came up to me. She had sparkly wings and a pink dress on. 'Hello, I need your help,' she said to me. 'A witch is going to make this land disappear!'

'Oh dear,' I said, 'that is bad,' and I agreed to help.

'Come this way.' She grabbed my hand and we flew off.

'This is high!' I said.

'I know, isn't it fun!'

'Err...yeah...it's fun,' I replied.

Then we landed. Everything was going dark. 'Oh dear,' said the fairy. 'She's making it dark now as well.

Just then a rabbit hopped out. I called it Lily and it hopped next to me. 'What's your name?' I asked the fairy.

'It's Rose. What's yours?' she asked back.

'My name is Annabel,' I said.

Finally we reached the witches castle. We sneaked through the window. We tiptoed up the stairs. We saw the witch but she saw us. We grabbed the bucket of water and threw it on the witch. She was gone.

Everyone was happy. 'Thank you!' cried Rose.

Annabel Johnson

'You're welcome,' I said and everyone was happy. The fairy waved her wand and we disappeared. I was back in my bed. I knew it was real because there was a wand in my hand.

Aleisha Rasool

I was trapped in a haunted house with spooky ghosts behind me. Bats were flying around with spiders crawling up me. Skeletons that were alive.

A baby was crying somewhere in the house. A scary zombie came. The zombie said, 'What's up darling?'

'I want my mummy,' said the baby skeleton.

'Aaahhhrrr, I've got you now!' said the scary zombie.

The baby skeleton screamed. He was fighting the scary zombie.

Just at that moment I woke up in my big comfy bed.

'Wow that was a scary nightmare!'

Freddie Gregson

One freezing afternoon there was someone called Jamie in my room. Suddenly, a door appeared. The cat said, 'Don't!' But Jamie went in.

The cat and Jamie were whizzing around. Just at that moment they went to Candy Land.

Jamie was so surprised. The cat put his head down in the ginger mud. He was stuck! Suddenly, a dinosaur smashed the candy building.

The cat heard the noise of a candy tree falling down. The dino took the cat, then Jamie shot the dino.

'BOOOOOOOOM!'

The cat was saved. Jamie was very hot. They happily teleported back to my room together.

Isaac Phelan

Have you ever thought you were dreaming because I will tell you what it's like. It all started on my seventh birthday and I was playing outside. Suddenly, BANG! A spaceship crash landed.

'Who are you?' I said to a little alien.

He took me to Food Land. Then I turned into a Sweet Super Hero. So I ate a gummy bear. Just at that moment candy cops arrested us.

Luckily, I still had my super powers. So with them I unlocked the doors. We ran outside quickly. The alien gave me a car that was as fast as a cheetah.

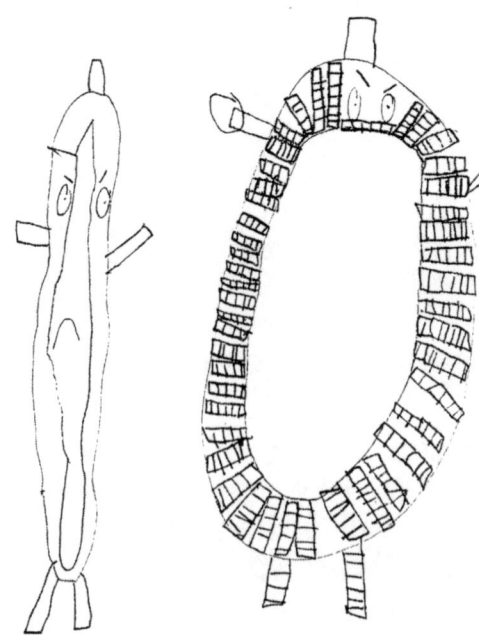

I kept the car a secret. Mum asked me why I was late. Just then the candy cops followed where I went. They knocked on the door. We didn't answer. Finally, they disappeared on that very day. I'm still waiting for my revenge!

Maddison Tew

One Sunday night I woke up in a Land of Zombies. Suddenly, they came out of their graves. They saw me and chased me. I was terrified and I wished I went home. It came true.

Was it was just a nightmare? I hoped! That is the scary bit of my life. I ran through the dark, gloomy graveyard and then into the dark, spooky, haunted wood. The zombies got lost but when I turned around there was a big, sloppy eyeball behind me!

Suddenly, I woke up in my bed and I looked in my pocket. There was the big, sloppy eyeball.

Year 3

THE THREE HEADED LION

O nce upon a time there lived a girl called Molly. She had a nightmare about a three headed lion that was made by a naughty wizard.

The lion chased Molly. She ran up the tree to get away. But the three headed lion had wings. Suddenly, the sun rose and blinded the lion and it fell to the ground. Molly ran away and never saw it again.

By: Sophie Strachan

THE NIGHTMARE AND DREAM SCHOOL

Once upon a time at school, a girl called Anna and a boy called Gary were playing. Suddenly, a big girl robot trashed the place.

'What should we do?' Gary asked Anna.

'Let's hide,' Anna replied.

'Okay.'

'It didn't work.'

'What now?'

'Arrrgggghhhheee,' Anna said for one minute.

They were thinking for an hour.

'Aha! Let's play with it,' Anna suggested.

It worked!

By: Stacy Wenlock

DREAMS AND NIGHTMARES

My nightmare is Father Christmas was ill and tried to get me! I ran and ran and I couldn't stop.

'Why is he trying to get me?'

'I'm evil. Is that all you can say?' said Father Christmas.

'Yes.'

I got away and huffed and puffed.

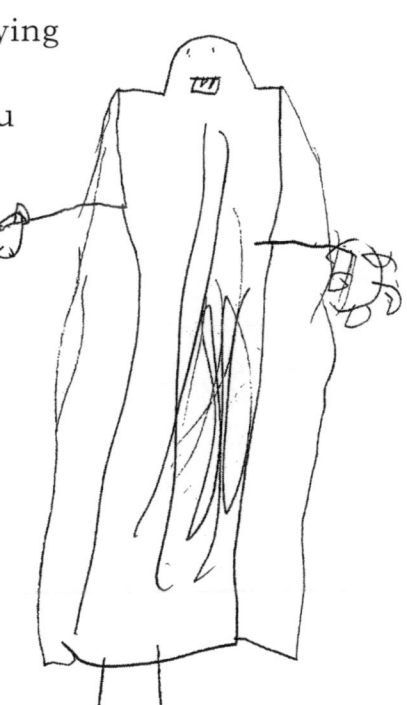

'This is a sword and a shield,' said a ghost, 'For killing the bad Father Christmas.'

He killed Father Christmas and lived happily ever after.

By: Alisha Deeney

CANDY LAND

I was in Candy Land. There was lolly trees of all sorts of sweets. Some funny sweet was there. That's not a sweet, that's Sweep the dog!

He leaves Sweep.

'What are you doing there?' I asked.

'I'm going to have to run here.'

'You can't leave your baby there!'

'Why?' asked Sweep.

'Your baby will eat all of the sweets.'

By: Lucy Atkinson

DREAM TO NIGHTMARE

One day a girl called Ruby had a dream. Suddenly, it turned into a nightmare. She wriggled around in bed. Then in her nightmare it got really scary.

She saw the scream and a cat with the scream as a face. She nearly woke up but she thought it's just a dream, it will get better. She did not know it was a nightmare.

A man came and offered her some candy. She took it. He pulled her. Can you guess what happened? Yes, she got kindnapped!

She got really sad. Her dream kept on changing. Slowly, she started crying. She really did not want to stay in that dream so she woke up. Then she said, 'It's just a dream,' and fell asleep.

By: Nicole Bowman

DREAM TO NIGHTMARE

One day a boy named Jerry was sleeping in the middle of the night when his closet opened. Jerry woke in such a fright. He looked at his closet and something came out.

It was a tentacle. It was black, red, pink, purple, brown, dark blue, blue, dark red, dark pink, light blue, violet, yellow and orange. It was covered in very gloopy slime. Then another tentacle and another and another. There were eight tentacles.

Jerry was very lucky he had a bunk bed. So he climbed the ladders and shouted for his mum. They came in as quick as a flash of lightning.

Mum screamed. Dad didn't. He went to his room, got a rope and lassoed the arms of the monster and sent it to a butcher. Every one was safe...for now!

By: Kyle Simpson

DREAM TO NIGHTMARE

O nce upon a time there was a man called Callum. He was bad. He knocked on people's doors and ran away. He was bad to a man. He killed him. But he knew not to.

One day he said sorry and then begged for money for a cancer charity but he spent it all on a house. He got arrested and then broke out of jail. So everyone looked for the escaped prisoner and then they found him. 'Why aren't you in prison?' they shouted. They locked him up.

By: Tia Perkins

THE CANDY DREAM

O nce in a house there lived a boy called Callum. His nickname is Callbosh. But who cares. One night I fell asleep and I had a dream and it started off pretty good actually.

'Race you! Ha! Ha!'

'BOOM!'

Wow! What was that? They went off in the direction where they heard the bang. Wow! They saw millions and millions of candys. Of course I called it Candy Land.

I called some of my friends to come and look. We thought it was neat so we went and had some candy. It was delicious actually. It was amazing!

Then we couldn't stop eating the candy. It was late at night when we felt sick so we just went home and went to bed.

lolly

sour sweet

twira

chocolate river

By: Callum Porter

HORROR CASTLE

Once upon a time there lived four boys. They were called Alex, Jude, Oliver and Riley. They were fishing. Then they found a castle. They went in.

Then they went through all the traps until they came to a room. The floor was gone. The floor was arriving. So were two monsters. They were thinking of a plan.

Then Alex jumps behind one of the monsters and stabs it in the back. He then stabbed the other one and they all went home.

By: Alex Benson

DREAM TO NIGHTMARE

'**G**ood afternoon son,' shouted Mum.

'Hi Mum,' replied Ben.

'Hi Dad,' said Ben.

'Hi Son,' replied Dad. 'What are we having for tea?' he shouted.

'Pepperoni Pizza,' yelled Mum.

'Mmmmmm,' said Dad.

'Thanks Mum,' yelled Ben.

'You're welcome,' shouted Mum.

'It's ready.'

'Coming,' said Dad and Ben.

...3 hours later.

'Tasty,' yelled Dad.

'Now Ben, time for bed,' said Mum in a stuffed way.

'Now Mum?'

'Yes.'

Then Ben fell asleep and had a nightmare.

He went to the forest and he heard a squeeky noise. It was getting louder. Suddenly, lots of glowing red rats appeared.

'Arrgh,' screamed Ben.

DREAM TO NIGHTMARE

Then lots of dirty giant rats chased him. They were so heavy that they were breaking the ground. Then the King of Rats came chasing me as well.

I could see lava and it was so hot it killed the rats. I stopped running and forgot about the lava and fell down, down and got killed by the lava.

By: Ben Turner

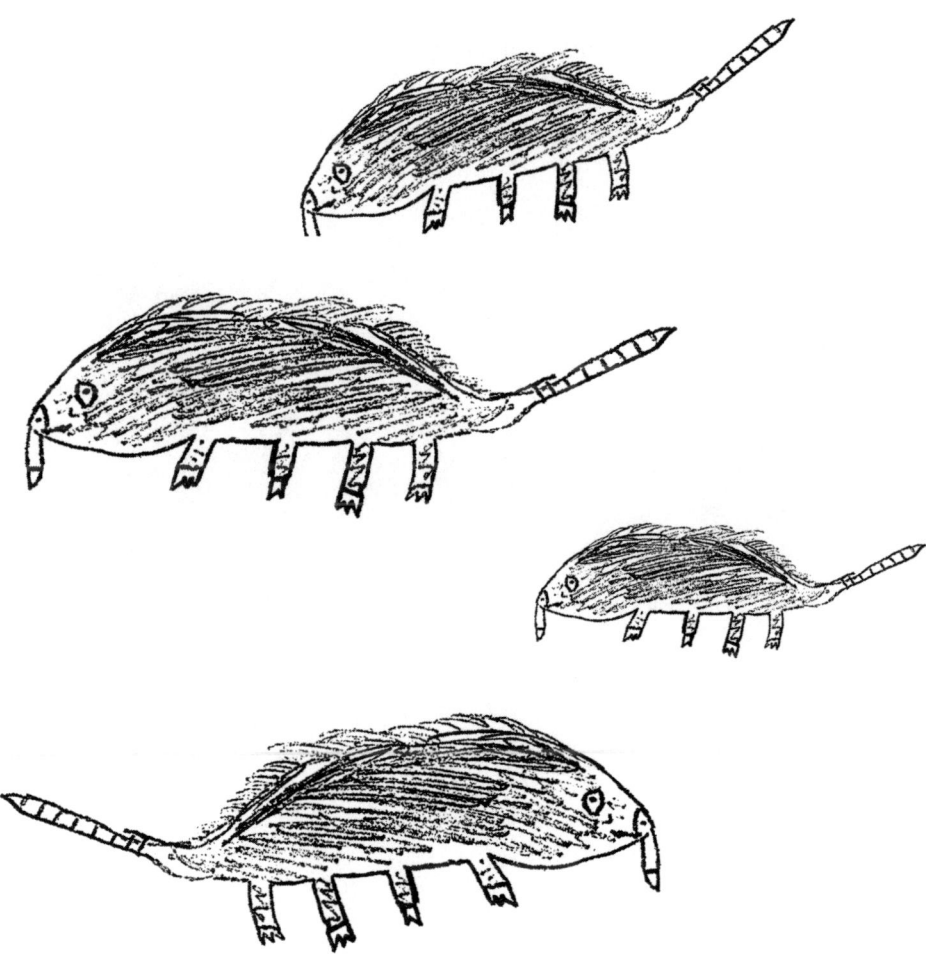

DREAM TO NIGHTMARE

Once there was a really nice man but he died. Everyone cried. But only one man didn't. But he had a tear in his eye. He went home and had his tea. He went to bed and he had a dream that he became a king. Then it turned into a nightmare.

Strangely, he woke up, went down stairs, had his breakfast and went to work. When he got home from work he got a new puppy and then he went to bed and had his dream again.

But this time he wouldn't wake up in the morning. So he knew he was in the dream. Then it turned into a nightmare that he turned into a monster. Then he woke up.

By: Ruby O'Connor

THIS CITY IS HAUNTED

I was on the beach asleep when a skeleton came with a knife. It was about to kill me when a guinea pig knocked the skeleton into the water with a splash!

When I looked back at the guinea pig I jumped on its back and it ran to a house. To my amazement the guinea pig said, 'Go inside. I'll be right next to you. Go in,' he said.

'Okay, okay,' I shouted.

So I went inside when I realised it was haunted. There were ghosts flying past, balls moving, tables spinning, vines down the walls and screaming noises!

We went into the house and the door slammed behind us. A black figure popped up in front of us.

"Let's get out.'

'How?'

'Err, jump out the window! 3..2..1..Go!

So we jumped out and ran away.

'That's quick thinking,' said the guinea pig. 'Thanks.'

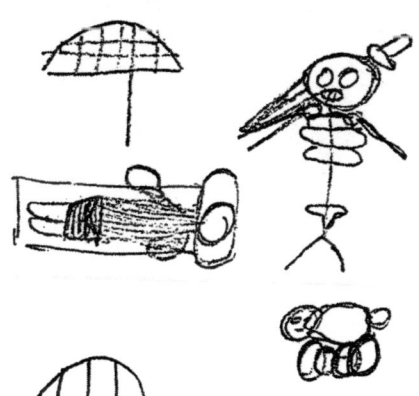

By: Jude Busby

HAUNTED HOUSE

Once I was having a party with Jude, Alex, and Ruby. When I was handing out cake.

'Who want's cake,' I said.

'Me,' replied Jude.

'Meeeeeee,' replied Riley.

So I gave out the cake. Then I gave out drinks. When I came to Alex, Eyeman came out.

'Aaaaagh,' shouted Riley.

Then suddenly Ben came in and shouted, 'It's hero time.'

Then me, Alex, Jude and Riley started to beat him up. Then Ben got thrown into the wall. The Judy got him

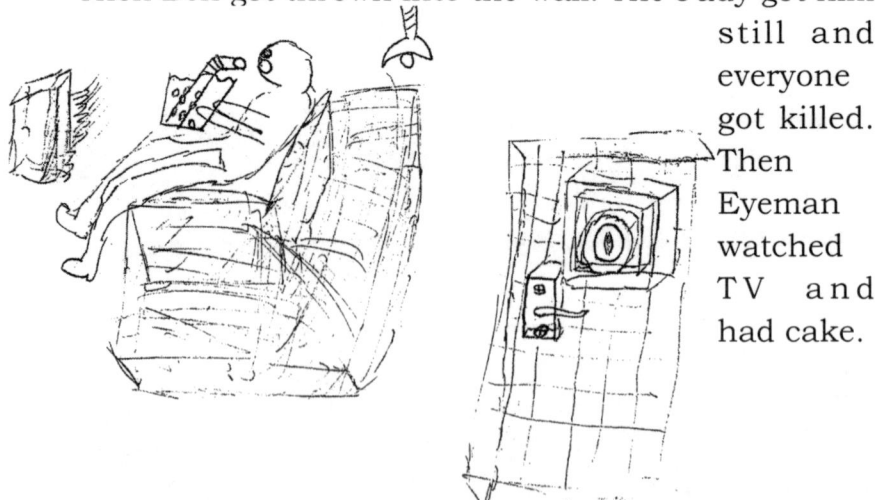

still and everyone got killed. Then Eyeman watched TV and had cake.

By: Oliver Harding

DREAM TO NIGHTMARE

O nce upon a time a really nice man died and instead of going to heaven he went to hell. He turned into a horrible man.

One day a teenager had a party. There was a knock at the door. Knock! Knock! Knock! Jasmine walked slowly to the door. Silently, she opened the door. There was a man wearing all black.

'Now I will kill you. Arrrrrrrrrr,' he said.

She was dead in an instant.

By: Faith Smith

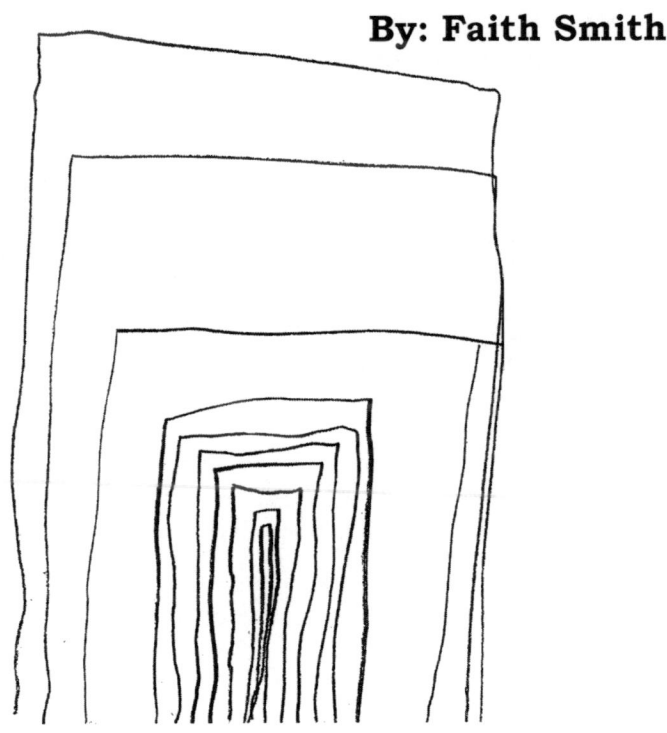

THE SPIKE ATTACK

Once upon a time Mr Brave was dreaming of nanobots dancing. Suddenly Dr Spike was there. It became a nightmare.

Mr Brave woke up. 'Is that real?' Mr Brave asked himself. He went to the window and peered out. 'Arrrrggghhh,' Mr Brave screamed. 'It is him.'

'Who?' said a voice.

'Who was that?' Mr Brave said.

Mr Brave turned around.

'Arrrggghhh,' Mr Brave said.

'I'm your mother. I have risen. Go get Mr Muscle he will help,' Mr Brave's mother replied.

'Mr Muscle?' Mr Brave shouted.

Mr Muscle lives in the flat below. He liked spending his time helping people.

'Yes Mr Brave,' Mr Muscle called.

'I need your help,' Mr Brave replied.

'Is it about Dr Spike?' Mr Muscle said calmly.

'Yep,' Mr Brave said. 'Can you go and kill some spikelings?'

'Yes,' said Mr Muscle.

'Thank you Mr Muscle. Here have this sword,' Mr Brave said.

'No thank you,' Mr Muscle said nicely.

THE SPIKE ATTACK

"Charge boys,' Mr Muscle shouted.

'Wait,' said Mr Brave bravely.

'Arrrggghhh,' screamed Mr Muscle.

'What was that sound?' said Mr Brave's mother.

Slowly, Mr Brave creeped to the window.

'Nanobots. I wonder who sent them? I know, it was Jason.'

Mr Brave's mother shouted, 'Hello. Everyone attack my nanobots, kill those spikelings. Crush them all! Leave no more! Ha, ha, ha, haaarrr.

'Thank you Jason,' shouted Mr Brave loudly.

By: Jett Tyler Donnelly

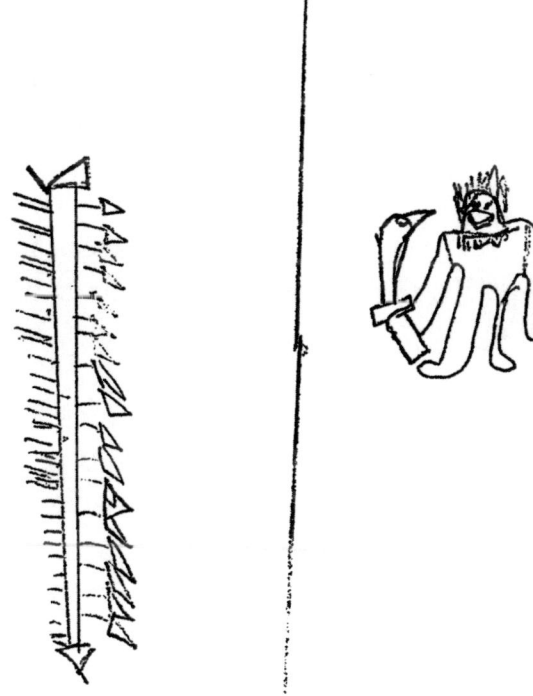

MIDNIGHT MEMORIES

One night a little girl called Bella and her twin sister Emily, went to bed. They shared bunk beds. Bella on top, Emily on the bottom. That's just a description now let's get to the story!

Once they got into bed Bella started to dream. It wasn't actually a dream it was a nightmare!

It started off like this. Bella landed on the floor in her room but Emily was gone so she went downstairs. Nobody was there. She heard footsteps coming down the stairs. She got worried. Meow! It was only her pet cat Ryan being silly.

Bella started to cry then she saw someone walking on the street with a bag, a very big bag. Her family were in there. The man kidnapped her and was never seen again...

Bella woke up with a scream and that's how the story ends!

By: Jessica Boughey

INDESTRUCTIBLE ISLAND

One day on indestructible island Padma and her little brother Indiana were lying on the sand. Suddenly a helicopter swooped over and some people came down a rope and pulled us into the helicopter.

We saw the inside and then darkness! One hour later we woke up to find ourselves strapped to iron beds! Suddenly, the ship exploded and we went home.

By: Jonas Leong-Smith

SOMETHING TERRIBLE

Once upon a time a man named Tom Stuart Pearlen was having a good dream about the world was ending. Then here's the good part. He got taken to heaven, met Jesus and Jesus turned Tom into an almighty angel.

Suddenly, he woke up in disgrace. He sat up. He looked at his clock it was 8:00 in the morning. 'Ugg. Why am I always late getting up?'

He walked down stairs. He had no wife or kids. he switched on the TV. He put on the news and made some breakfast.

'What should I have? Cherios, cornflakes. I'll have cornflakes.'

SOMETHING TERRIBLE

Now it was midnight. He fell asleep but he had a nightmare about the world ending. Then he goes to hell and somebody turns Tom into a monster!

A couple of days after he knew at 9:00pm at midnight he turns into a terrible monster and he has been praying for the spell to go away.

One day his fairy god mother comes and uses her wand and with a word, Abracadabra Zipty Babra, the spell goes away. And they lived happily ever after ..but not for long!

By: Jessica Louise Wallbank

DREAM TO NIGHTMARE

O nce upon a time I went to one of the first class hotels. I went on the dance floor, dancing to the music until half past twelve, so just past midnight.

I went up the stairs where they were decorated in beautiful red and gold coloured carpet. There were loads of paintings on the wall.

Firstly, I got up the fifty steps. After that I got 20 pence and paid to go in the shower. Things were going well...'Ahh...that was nice.' After that I went to bed.

Suddenly, a smash came from the window. A person jumped into the room and took my wallet and the 24 carat gold bracelet. Then I went for the door and told the police that were standing right outside the hotel door.

The police ran up the stairs gasping for breath and then...I woke up! I realised it was just a dream and outside was sunny. So I went outside to play.

By: Kristian Worsley

DREAM TO NIGHTMARE

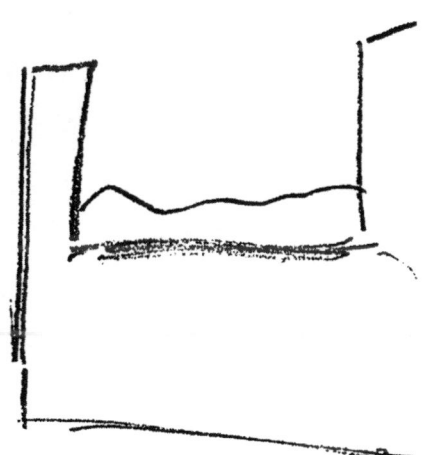

DREAM TO NIGHTMARE

Once upon a time there was a boy who dreamed to get a dog. The next night he screamed because a monster ripped his head off with his monster friend, a fire breathing dog dragon with a rat tail.

A week after at school, boys were beating him up and hitting him and the dog he dreamed of was getting beaten up by monsters. The monsters were laughing.

Suddenly, the dog vanished. A different dog came and turned the monsters to ash and jelly. We ate all the jelly. It was apple. It was tasty and fresh.

By: James Bates

SLENDERMAN

I was in a dark and gloomy forest then I noticed a sign and it said...

COLLECT ALL
EIGHT PAGES
AND YOU CAN
ESCAPE!

'Eight pages!?!' I thought. Then I looked in a box and got out a torch, turned it on and I searched for the eight pages in the woods.

It took me eight minutes to find them but then I saw... Slenderman! I suddenly was teleported onto a beach. It was happy and sunny. The children were playing and then ice cream dropped into my hand.

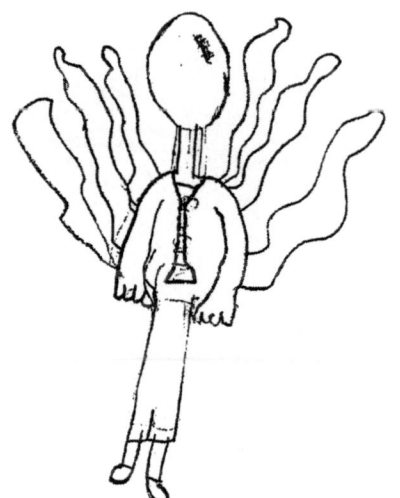

Once I'd finished it I heard a voice it said, 'Wake up! Wake up!' It was my little sis. Then I told her what a dream I had and it was a bit of a nightmare!

By: Bronwyn Kerr

THE MISSING CAKES

My dream is me having a face made out of cakes and H.E.R.O.B.R.I.N.E. He has a tiny cake. Now it turns into my nightmare! H.E.R.O.B.R.I.N.E takes all of my cakes and turns some into little ones and I, Popylerammos think, 'What!? Nooooooooooo...' and H.E.R.O.B.R.I.N.E thinks, 'Muahahahaaaaaa'.

By: Dylan Pilkington

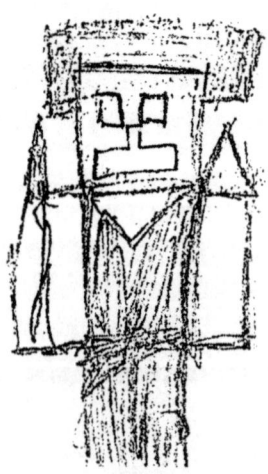

DREAM TO NIGHTMARE

In my dream I was in a land of candy. I was licking a candy cane. I have paws to help me. Then a person appeared to give it to me and we shook hands and I woke up!

By: Morton Hendren

THE HAUNTED CASTLE

One day there were four toys called Alex, Jude, Oliver and Riley. They were walking along a big field. They had never been half way across that field.

The next day was Saturday and they had more time to go outside. Then Jude thought of a plan. It was that they could go all the way across the field. Everybody said yes.

Ten minutes later they arrived at the field. Then they set off. They brought five biscuits each in case they got hungry on the way. Later they got across and they had eaten their biscuits. It led to a dark, scary forest.

Riley just ran and ran through the darkness until... click...Riley ran to a tree and hid behind it. Then his friends came. 'You scared me,' said Riley. Then they started adventuring.

Soon they found a creature. They was all scared so they waited a bit. Bang! It was thunder so they all went inside. There were two big scary creatures so they spilt up.

Oliver went with Jude and I went with Alex. I was really strong, Alex had a sword, Oliver had fireballs and Jude had a whip.

Later, Oliver and Jude found a room of ghostly creatures. Riley and Alex found the room and came in.

THE HAUNTED CASTLE

There was an extra door so they opened it at the same time.

'Ahhhh!' they all said. It was a room full of echoes. Later they went back downstairs and found out that there was a downstairs room that they went to explore.

'Let's go in there,' said Oliver.

'Yes, but you go first,' answered Jude.

They went in there and then Alex, Riley and Oliver fell in a trap and got eaten. Jude ran away but got trapped and then eaten. Their parents were worried where they were so they followed in their footsteps and the same thing happened to them!

By: Riley Choularton

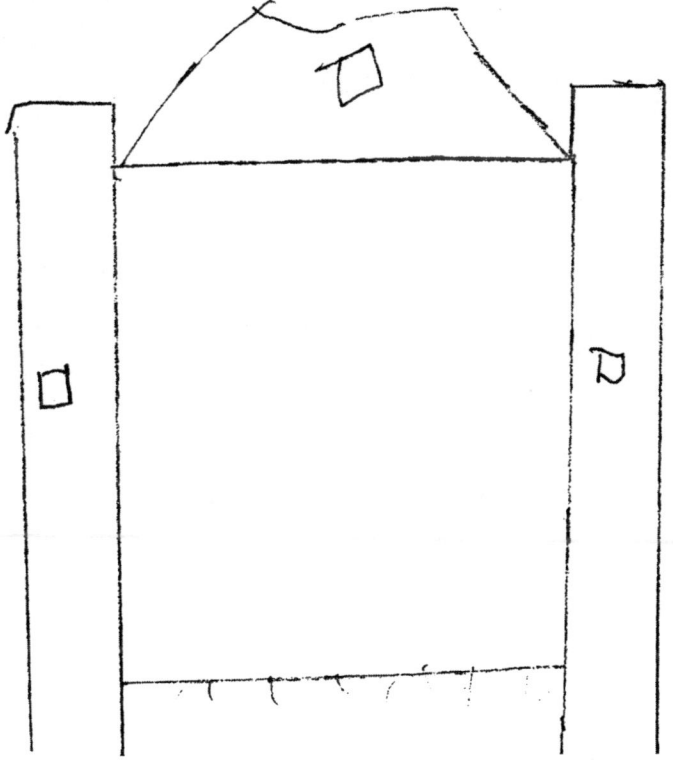

THE PEPSI MAX OF TERROR

I was in Blackpool stood next to the Pepsi Max rollercoaster. I was too small to go on the ride and felt angry. I wandered off to find something to eat and found a Burger King. A turkey sandwich looked good so I ordered it.

Walking back to the rollercoaster I ate my sandwich when suddenly my legs grew longer. I went to check if I was tall enough to go on the ride. 'Yipee! Hooray! I'm so happy!' I shouted as I realized I could go on the rollercoaster.

Queueing up made me feel excited and I finally saw the carriages coming down the track. I jumped quickly into the back carriage and watched the bar come down. The rollercoaster started to move. 'I've changed my mind!' I screamed but it was too late to come back.

The rollercoaster climbed to the top of the dip when suddenly the bar snapped and I tumbled out. 'Arrrggghhh! Help me!' I fell downwards but luckily the rollercoaster turned into a pile of fluffy quilts so I landed safely. That was a close one!' I thought to myself.

By: Daniel Carpenter

Year 4

Haikus

Vampire

 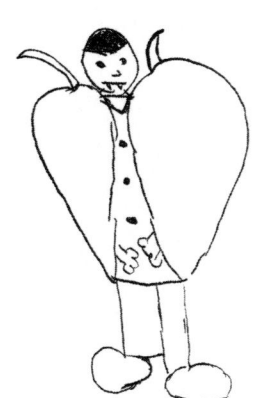

The midnight creeper.
The midnight zone blood
sucker.
A beastly killer.

Billy Hutchinson

Zombies

They walk through the
graves.
They always creep up on
you.
They are so gruesome.

Tom Michie

 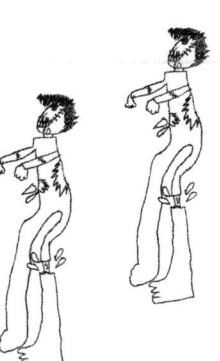  

Puppies

The cute small puppies.
The puppies were playing
good.
Fetching and catching.

Leah Parr

The Hand Ripper

The hand comes at night!
You can't see him when
it's bright.
It gives you a fright!

Jake Satterley

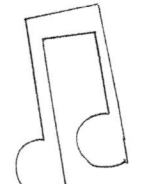

My Dream

Dancing to the beat.
Taking selfies with I.D.
Until it's half past three.

Zoë Naylor

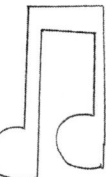

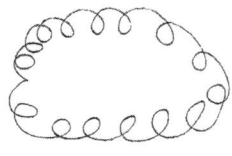

Candy Floss Clouds

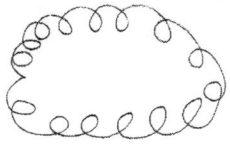

Fluffy and poofy.
Chewy and brightly
coloured.
Sticky ginormous.

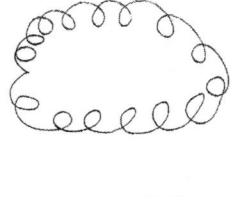

Jessica Clements

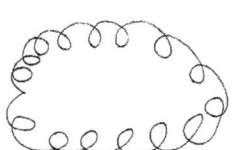

125

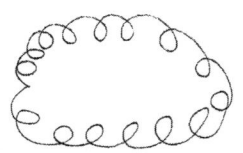

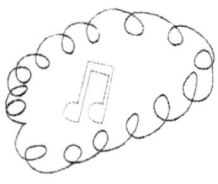 

Chocolate

I love all the taste.
I like chocolate it is nice.
I find it lovely.

Luke Akrigg

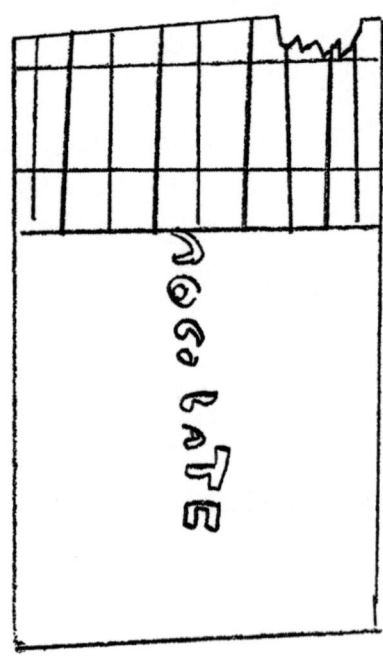

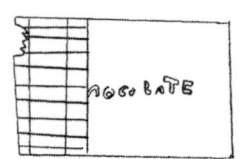

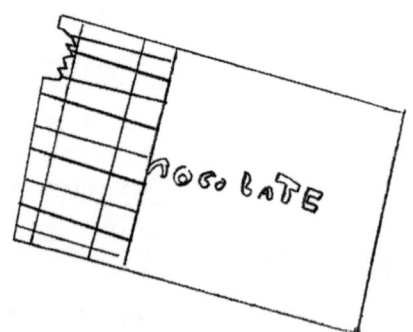

Games

I want to make games.
I want to work for EA.
It will be great fun.

Owain Kirkbride-Duckett

Fairies

Fairies are shiny.
Fairies are in a meadow.
Fairies on the grass.

Grace Swallow

127

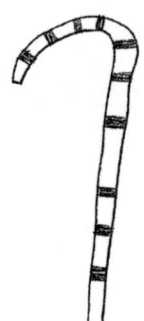
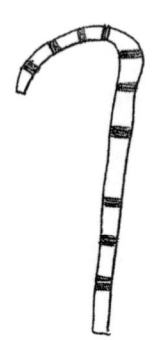

Sweet Land

I look all around.
Everything is made of
sweets.
The sun is sherbert.

Alicia-Anne Mason

Paleontology

White and brown colours.
Paleontology fun.
White and mouldy bones.

Amber Rutherford

Godzilla

He's loud and evil.
He eats humans for his
lunch.
Scary Godzilla.

Alex Davis

Bones

Rattle in the night.
Eyes hollow, black and empty
Flesh turned into dust.

Aston Porter

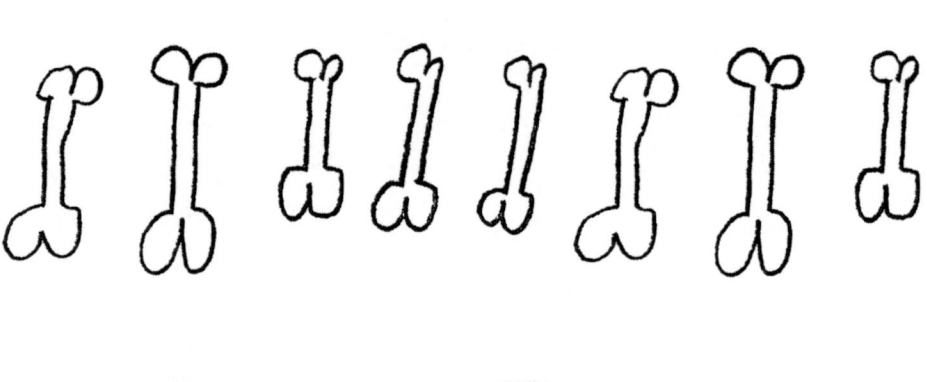

KƎNNiNgS PoƎMS

Enderman

As tall as a tree.
As black as the night sky,
A really hard monster to kill.
A very sneaky monster,
In the minecraft world.

Dante Okwiri

The Gingerbread Man

Hot from the oven,
Smells warm and inviting.
Golden and brown,
Tastes mouth wateringly good.
First an arm, then a leg,
Last of all bite off his head.

Layton Hudson

Zombie

Human slayer.
Grave yard liker.
Home invader.
Undead wanderer.
Brain eater.

Harry Atkin

A Bat

A dusk waker.
A swift flyer.
An insect eater.
A black stalker.
A night lover.
A blood sucker.

Leo Mackintosh

Minecraft

Shoots an arrow its from a game.
It's white it's made of bones.
It is very annoying, it can kill you.
It's a mold!
Lives in a cave, very scary!

Callum Budden

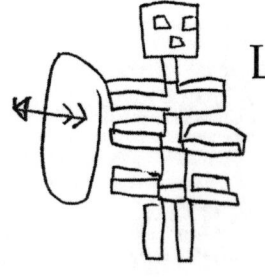

Rock Climber

As strong as a bull.
No gear.
Daring and
dangerous.
Wears safety gear.
Going through a...

...path of falling
rocks.
Climbing to
heights
no one should
think of.

Isabel Mary Rigby

Music Land

Very enthusiastic people,
Dancing to the beat.
Always have their headphones on,
Joyful when they listen.
A band won't be made without them,
Loves to play instruments.

Shannon Paige Pilkington

Gingerbread Man

It is very sweet.
It shouldn't smile because it will die.
Has no hair but is ginger.
Paralysed because of us.
Loves his colourful buttons
and is in a fairy tale.

Matthew Smail

A Vampire

A blood sucker.
Lives in a graveyard.
Likes to fly.
Human Hunter.

Ruby Birkett

A Vampire

As tall as a drainpipe.
As pale as paper.
Eyes as red as blood.
A blood sucker.
Some sharp fangs.

Alfie Morris

Agents

They are prison senders.
Brave heroes.
Gun shooters.
Good friends.
Bad stoppers.
Top secret.
Black uniform.
Deadly people.

Joshua Lefever

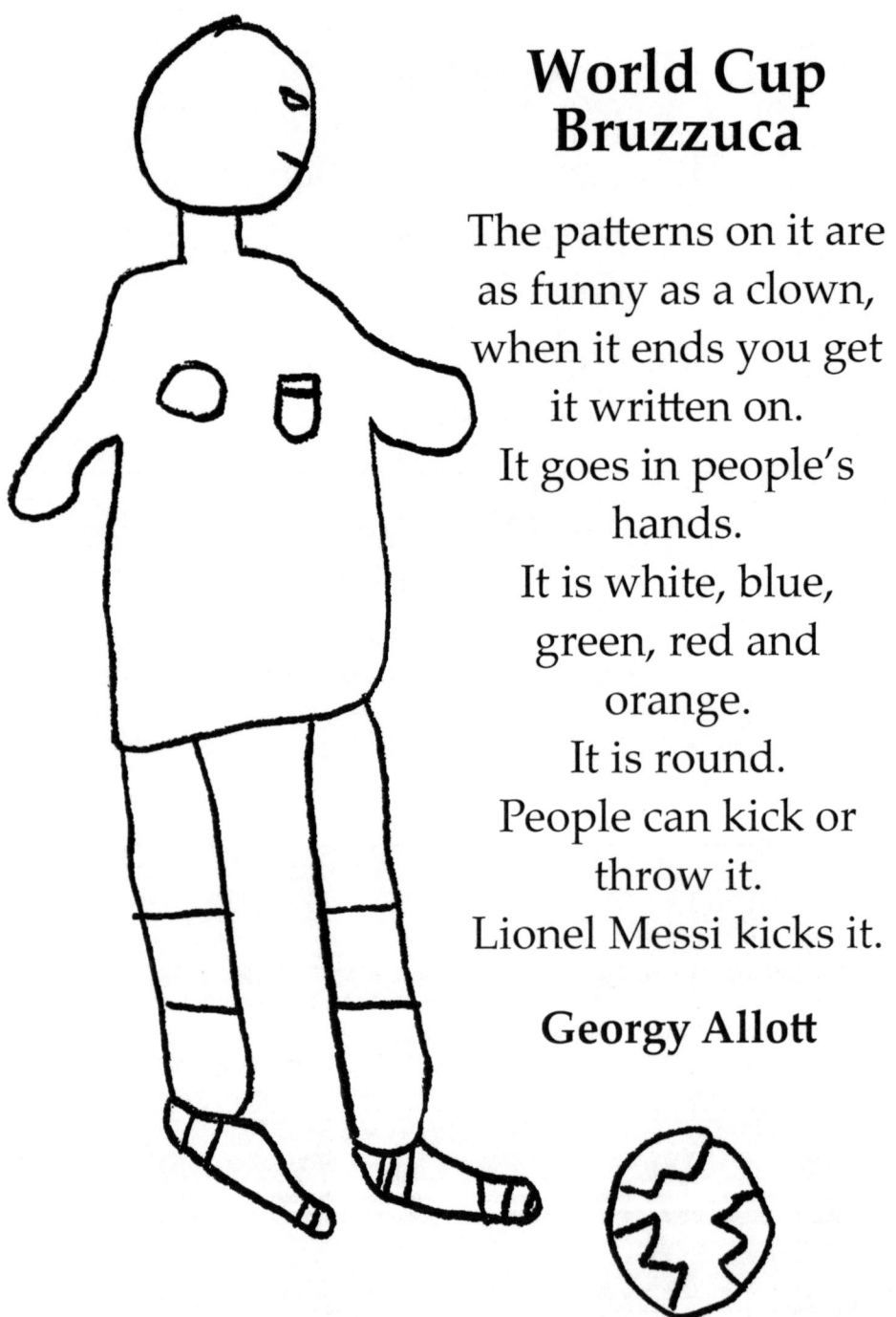

World Cup Bruzzuca

The patterns on it are
as funny as a clown,
when it ends you get
it written on.
It goes in people's
hands.
It is white, blue,
green, red and
orange.
It is round.
People can kick or
throw it.
Lionel Messi kicks it.

Georgy Allott

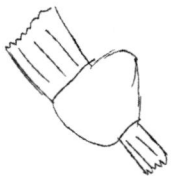

Toffee

As small as paper.
Good and sticky.
Chewy as chewing gum.
Brown in a packet.
Different shapes and sizes,
laughing in the sun.

Chloe Davidson

A Pony

It always has racing competitions.
It makes a noise when it moves.
You have it as a pet,
and it lives in a stable.

Anya Dean

A Helicopter

As heavy as a boulder.
As colourful as sand.
Manhandled inside.
As hard as a brick.
Bigger than a car.
It flies like a bird.

Logan Robertson

Amazing Gymnast

As amazing as a shooting star.
As colourful as a rainbow.
A great jumper like a kangaroo.
A fantastic balancer.
They can do tricky stuff like a diver.
A beautiful cart-wheeler.
A wonderful roller.
A good person who can do the splits.

Molly Livermore

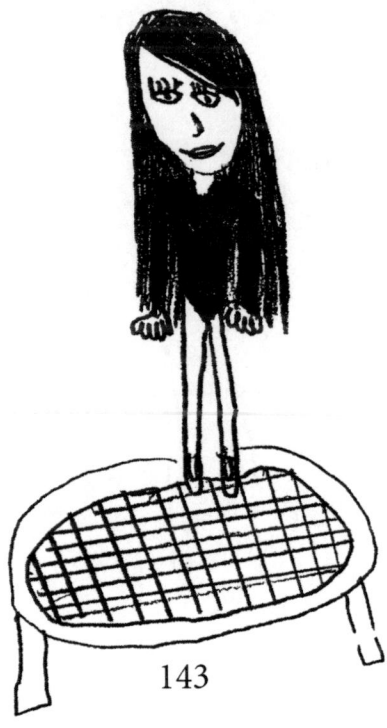

Tiger Pet

As orange as the sun.
As stripy as a zebra.
It has got fluffy fur.
Nice and gentle with me,
my friends and family.
Really fast.
It is a type of animal.
He eats meat.
Scares!

Jake Sprules

Francesco Gardiner

'Arrghh...' came a distant scream, which made Toby and Luigi want to turn back. But they weren't about to leave an enormous, historic jackpot. They stepped into the house. The house was nearly five hundred years old. As

they entered the house they saw and heard a strange creature in the window which creeped him out a little.

The stared at the gigantic, mouldy staircase, each step creaked loudly. Suddenly, as they walked past the landing doors a moan came from within the eighth room. There was a throne in the middle of the room.

Katy Atkinson

Long ago when ghosts were around people were scared of them. One day a young lady was walking by a funny looking house. The young lady did not know that a ghost was following her. She ran and ran and ran but it was too late the poor young lady was killed forever.

Her husband walked past and said, 'Oh no!' The ghost was following behind him. 'Oh no! Help!'

He ran and ran and ran. Luckily he found a house. He went into a room. Suddenly, ghosts were everywhere but the man did not know that they had tried to kill him. They didn't.

'Wow! He is amazing. We shall turn him into a ghost. Years from now the ghosts were walking on the street with their new one. But they had a girl ghost too. Not one girl ghost but two girl ghosts. The man looked at them. The ghosts killed the man.

'Aaaarrrggghhh!' Gone forever just like his wife!

Ethan Livesey

There were two boys called John and Peter both aged 9. One day they were playing. The bushes rattled. They looked but it had run off. So they went looking. They found a field with a dead cow in it. They ran back home. That night something opened the gate.

'What if it's the beast?' John said.

'Let's go and have a look,' said Peter.

'Ok,' answered John.

So they went on the back garden and found something. Then fog rolled in and it vanished…so they went back to bed.

The next day everybody came out and then John and Peter told everybody. The next night they found out where it lived. They went in and someone pushed the door and it creaked closed behind them. They couldn't get out. It moved faster.

It got John but Peter ran. More of the creature came out. It had horns, three eyes and two tongues. It was red. It had a massive fist that had rock on it and it breathed fire.

'Join us John and kill Peter,' said the creature.

Ethan Livesey

So they killed him and there were guts everywhere. Then they went after his mum. After that many monsters came back to live and they took over the world. They went to war again and all the monsters and humans were dead.

Kyran Rodgerson

I always dreamt about sleeping over at my friend's house. I brought two Fredo's, one KitKat, a game, a game book and a toothbrush. I had thought wrong! The house was black. It had a double door and two scary towers. However, the sky was all dark. There were no stars. It was pitch black.

I heard a voice getting closer and closer. Someone grabbed my shoulder. I don't know who it was, but someone. I turned around. He or she disappeared in the dark. I went back the next day but this time I was prepared for battle if I had to.

I saw it. It was a bog. He was a ghost. He dragged me to the stairs in the house and he disappeared. He said his name was Bob!

Every stair creaked. I froze in terror and heard frightful noises from the towers.

Matthew Foot

Quietly, Bobby went across the unstable bridge to get to his house. He saw his house but it looked unusually strange. It sent a shiver down his spine. He grabbed hold of the doorknob very slowly and stepped in carefully. He went in the kitchen very slowly blowing away the cobwebs. He looked at the cooker and said, 'I might have something to eat!'

Then he opened a cupboard. Suddenly, two tarantulas jumped out trying to attack him. Then a trapdoor opened and he fell through the floor. Bang! He hit the floor. Then when he woke up he heard mumbling. He saw his best friend tied up above a lava pit. He was really scared now.

Then a massive mutant zombie came. 'Brainzzz,' screeched the zombie. He friend threw him a gun. He picked up the gun but he had no ammo. Then the zombie charged at him. The zombie fell over and fell into the lava pit. He untied his friend and they climbed out of the trapdoor and escaped the dark and evil house.

Matthew Foot

Spencer Thompson-Eccles

I've been dreading the day that go in the old house by the sea. It had been there for hundreds of years, just sat there and no one had ever been near it…not until today.

I started to walk over. I got to the gate and opened it. The gate is very rusty and covered in ivy from top to bottom.

I walk towards the house. Suddenly, I shrieked as something hit the ground. A figure was standing there. When I walked towards it it was gone. Nervously, I walked in shivering not because it was cold, although it was rather cold, but because I was terrified.

The house was very black. I felt something watching me as I climbed the endless tower. There were holes everywhere and I got that creepy feeling that someone was watching me. I got to the top to see the figure standing there staring at me but its ghost state threw me. I turned around and it was gone.

Sonny Whiteside

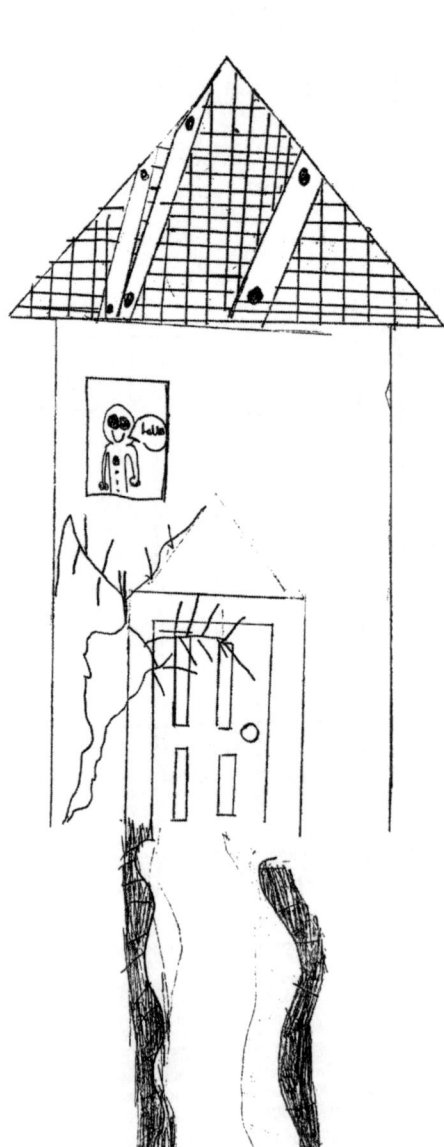

The moment I drove past the old wispy cottage by the forest I knew that something or someone was in there. I put my brakes on. The very thought of, 'Should I go in?' I grabbed my keys and got out. The feeling in my feet was horrible, trembled as I stood still staring at the cottage. Then I heard the uncanny noise of a groaning woman. It came from the cottage. As I ran to the door a voice said, 'It's done. The transformation is complete.'

I started running

towards the house. I knew I shouldn't have opened the door but with a big GULP I charged in, recklessly intruding.

The lights flickered. My body froze, my arms paralysed. I managed to stop trembling. The abandoned house started to shake.

'Help!'

Nobody heard me.

'Escaping is the wrong way. Stay, live, be free,' said the little voice again.

The creepiness was unreal. I started to climb the stairs so slowly that I was quieter than a pin-drop. I went up one by one, then…

The ghosts appeared. I pegged it out of the house and jumped in my car and drove off.

'Get up,' said my mum as she woke me from my slumber.

'I had a terrible nightmare last night,' I said.

'Tell me all about it later,' said mum softly.

Toby Brown

Returning to my old house made me feel strange after so many years. I walked slowly to the iron gate which had been rusted by all the salt water. Slowly, I snapped the ivy stems to get through the gate, which the ivy was almost strangling. Then I stopped. I looked at the house. A split second later an, 'Ooooohhhhh!' came from inside the brick building and a white shadow went past the highest window.

'What was that?' I thought, and I stepped inside.

I got inside and looked around. It was terrifying! There were rats, bats and spooky hats. I slowly and nervously creaked my way upstairs.

Quietly, I opened the door in the middle of the hall. Then I realised I was not prepared for what I was about to face. !!GHOSTS!!. But not just two or three, oh no! There were hundreds of them!

Toby Brown

Joseph Magowan

I always dreamt of going back home. Living with other people is not fun. When I got home it was not my home. There were church like windows but I knew it was not a church. The gate was creepy when I went up to it. It creaked. Then I saw a ghost.

The ghost said, 'Come inside if you dare.'

I went inside slowly. The stairs creaked. There were tons of stairs. When I went into a room a ghost jumped at me. 'Arrrggghhh!' I shouted. I just carried on. Walking slowly I opened the door to go into the next room. There was the very same ghost that I saw in the first room so I thought there was something really freaky. When I went to the top I saw...I saw a gimongous giant ghost!

'I am the biggest giant and I am going to kill you,' he said.

Joseph Magowan

163

Ashley Robinson

Today I am returning home…Turning down the bumpy road I start to see the house. When I get out I go in. When I go up the steps of the house the door opened by itself. I slowly entered.

There are cobwebs on the wall, a bit on the floor and the door is covered with cobwebs. All of the furniture is covered in cobwebs and the light has loads on. I creep slowly up the stairs and every time I step on a step the staircase creaks.

When I reach the top of the stairs I go into my room and there is someone or something in my bed. I slowly walk over to my bed and pull the duvet off and it is a Teddy Bear! I was so scared I thought it was a ghost!

I go into another room and I see a cute little doll. I pick it up and it says, 'Hiya,' and turns its head around and stares at me. I scream and throw it across the room.

Ashley Robinson

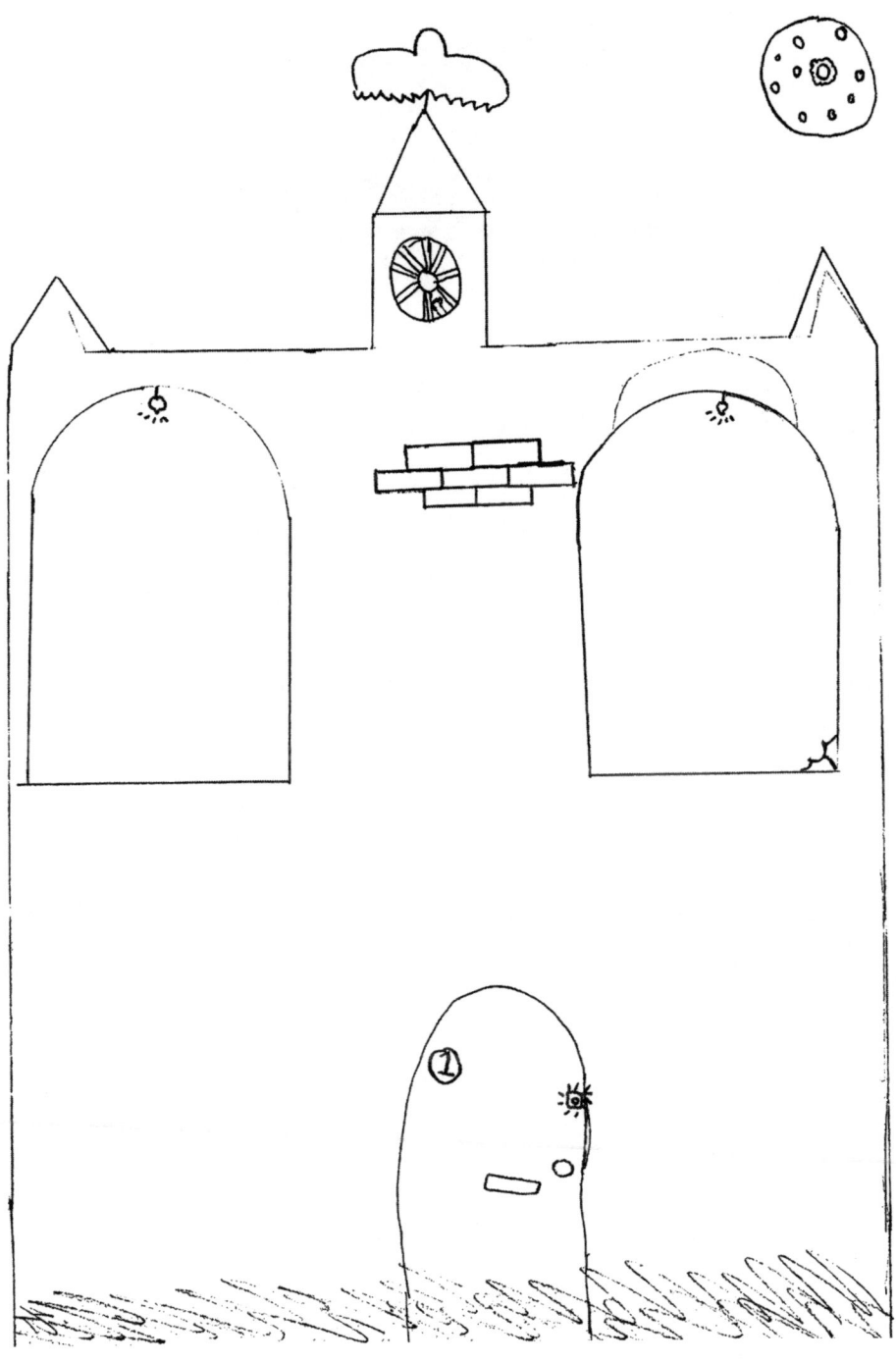

165

Olivia Mae Cartledge

I tremble walking up to the house, the wind blowing me back as the sun is going down. The house has a massive tower. The tower is swaying from side to side. I open the gate covered in ivy. It creaks open. I am trembling. I knock on the door. Bang! Bang! Bang! The brown door creeeaks open. Creeping inside I can see the long staircase.

Walking to the staircase I'm dreading it. I see a strange shadow moving across the room. I get even quieter. There was a flash of light. There was a g...g... ghost!

'BOO!'

I fainted.

When I woke up I wasn't okay with the figure. I screamed and ran away and when I got in the garden I fell. I quickly ran away...

The next day I came back to the spooky house and crept up the stairs again and I saw it!

Olivia Mae Cartledge

Harrison Baird

There was a big mansion with black paintings everywhere on the outside of this mansion. I was very desperate to go inside but it was too creepy on the outside of the house!

So then, I went into the house. The door slowly creaked open. I stepped in a bit! All I heard was, 'Oooooh, oooooh, oooooh!' I was petrified.

I had to go upstairs, so I went up. The stairs were HUGE! The stairs on the left went right up to the top of this huge mansion. I went up the stairs on the right first. When I eventually got to the top there were about twenty rooms. I stepped forward and the floor fell through but luckily I jumped back. I had to jump across the hole.

The room had lots of instruments but then I heard, 'Ohhhohhhaaarrrrgh.' All the other rooms were empty. I went up the stairs on the left. When I got to the top there was a choir going on.

'So, all these sounds were you guys singing?!'
'YES!'

Katie Lamb

As I was returning to my house after I had been away for a couple of years. I was frozen to the spot. My jaw dropped because I looked up slowly and saw…Ivy strangling the house as if the sea had coated the walls in salt. Next I looked at the fence that was surrounding my house. It was covered in dark green moss. I couldn't look at the house anymore. I tried to run away as fast as I could but the house dragged me in.

'No! Don't go. I have a lot more to show you!' it said as if it was grumbling in a mean voice.

Stopping, I thought about it a bit more. Accidentally, I let out a ginormous SCREAM!

I nervously crept along the front garden amongst all the patches of grass that were fading away one by one. As I was trembling I opened the front door quickly. As quick as a flash the door slammed behind me like someone wanted to keep me. The slam made me jump so I held onto a wooden post and put my finger in a huge spider cobweb. I looked up at the staircase that led to an old bedroom.

Suddenly, at the top of the stairs there was a dark

shadowy figure looking directly at me. Blinking again, the creepy figure had disappeared.

Calmly, I started to make my way up the steps. As soon as I stepped on the first one it creaked and so did every single other one until…I got to my old bedroom.

I opened the door. I peered around my room. All the paint and wallpaper had fallen off. My bed was in millions of pieces. I wasn't more scared in all my life. I tried to run away but the door slammed and locked itself. I was trapped.

Eve Painter

Returning to my Nanny's house I slowly opened the old rusted gate which made a loud creak deafening me. I walked cautiously towards the wooden door but it was already open. I stepped slowly into the big gloomy room. I called out to see if anyone was there but no answer. I tiptoed upstairs but I guessed it would be hopeless because my nanny wasn't very good at

getting around. But I guessed it would be worth a shot if I wanted to find her.

'Who's there?' called a muffled voice.

'Nanny?' I replied.

'Oh! Hello dearie. You remember me. Do you still visit my grave?'

'But Nanny, you're not dead.'

I stopped and froze and then realised my nanny was a ghost!

'Aaaaaaaah!'

I ran down the stairs but my nanny was chasing me. She wore a bleached white nightie and her skin was white and pale. Her hair was grey and curled and had a little bow on the front. Her face was old and wrinkled. She certainly looked...Dead! I reached the door but it was locked. She reached out to grab me but missed. I read that the way to kill a spirit was to re-jig her memory.

I thought of her cat, Tinkles. There he was a living black and white cat.

'Nanny, do you remember Tinkles? He's your cat. You loved him and fed him. I used to come round and wouldn't let go of him. He loves you and I know you love him so please remember. Please, please, please, because you're my nanny and I'm your granddaughter.

Eve Painter

I am human not a ghost.'

Slowly her skin got it's colour back and her voice went normal again. I glimpsed and saw a plaque saying, Trapville Castle.

'Nanny, what does that mean?'

'Oh? You don't know? Well when you are in here you are trapped like all of us. He, he, he.'

'Aaarrrggghhhhh...'

But no one can hear you scream.

Harvie Busby

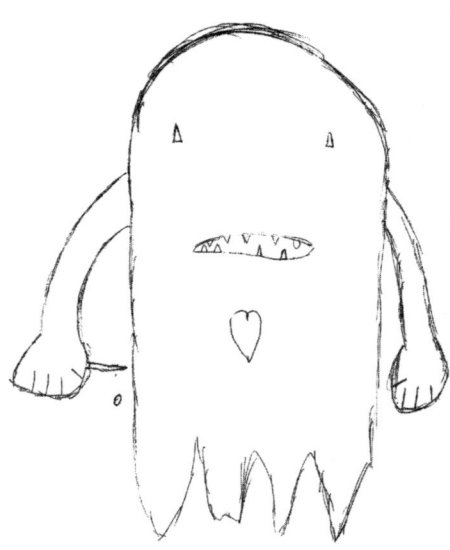

I always

wanted to go back to my old house. So the day was today. I gently pushed the gate open until I came to a halt.

I saw a figure in the window, a tall one with a long beard. I carried on pushing on the gate. There he was again in the other window. Then I came to the door. I was just about to knock and the door opened itself. I stared around. No one was safe there…

I stepped inside and crept up the stairs. They were steep and quiet at the top. A wolf howled and pushed me back down onto a scorching HOT fire with mobs of people around prepared to eat me. There were ten zombies, twenty skeletons, ten spiders and twenty vampires.

'Arrrggghhh!'

Nathan Torkington

One day I dreamed of becoming a fairground helper and working for the horror part and it came true. One day I went in it because nobody was in there anymore and nobody ever came out of it. I did not find it scary at all but I saw a ghost so I went back in and did not stay.

Nathan Torkington

A few days later nobody was going. So I went in again and I saw the ghost but it was a different ghost. I never went back in again.

'Can I work on the bumper cars?' I said to my boss.

'Yes,' he said.

So I did. Loads of people went on and nobody crashed into each other. I thought it was a bit weird but I just did my job. I could not go on the bumper cars because loads of people went on them. After a while people stopped going on them so I finally went on them.

I let go of the steering wheel and it went left rather than straight on.

'I can't work here anymore,' I said to my boss, 'I can't because this place is haunted!'

Charrelle Porter

I always knew I would come back. I have lovely dreams about it but sometimes I have terrible nightmares. It has finally come. I'm at the house and the gates are all rusty from the salty sea coming in over the horizon. It looks so beautiful...but mysterious.

I walk towards the gate trembling. I look up and I see a strange figure in the window in the tallest tower. I blinked and it suddenly disappeared. I wanted to run away but I couldn't. The gate slammed shut. It really scared me.

I carefully opened the creaky door. I stepped in and the lights started flickering. I could hear footsteps up and down the stairs and the worst thing of all is the figure. Every time I blinked I saw it but it was a different figure every time. This time it was more serious.

I crept up the stairs very quietly. It happened again, just before I opened the door. I saw the creepiest one... POW! I got knocked out by a secret doorway.

Charrelle Porter

Miles Choularton

I always dreamed of returning to the house. There it was sitting there waiting for its first victim. Well, I'm going to the house to see what's inside. I walked up to the metal gates with shivers down my spine.

I touched the gate and it opened. It made a screechy noise. Just at that moment I saw a black figure in the window of the tallest tower. I looked away for a second then it was gone.

I walked towards the door and it creepily opened. The spooky house was full of cobwebs. Then I saw the biggest stairs of my life. I walked up the stairs very slowly. I was scared. Right in front of my eyes I saw a white person fly across the air into the tallest tower.

I slowly walked into the room. That very moment I saw something that I had never seen before. I froze. I ran out of the house. It sucked me back in. The monster was a three headed dragon. It had sharp teeth and poison. I had to do something about this. But I didn't know what to do...

Miles Choularton

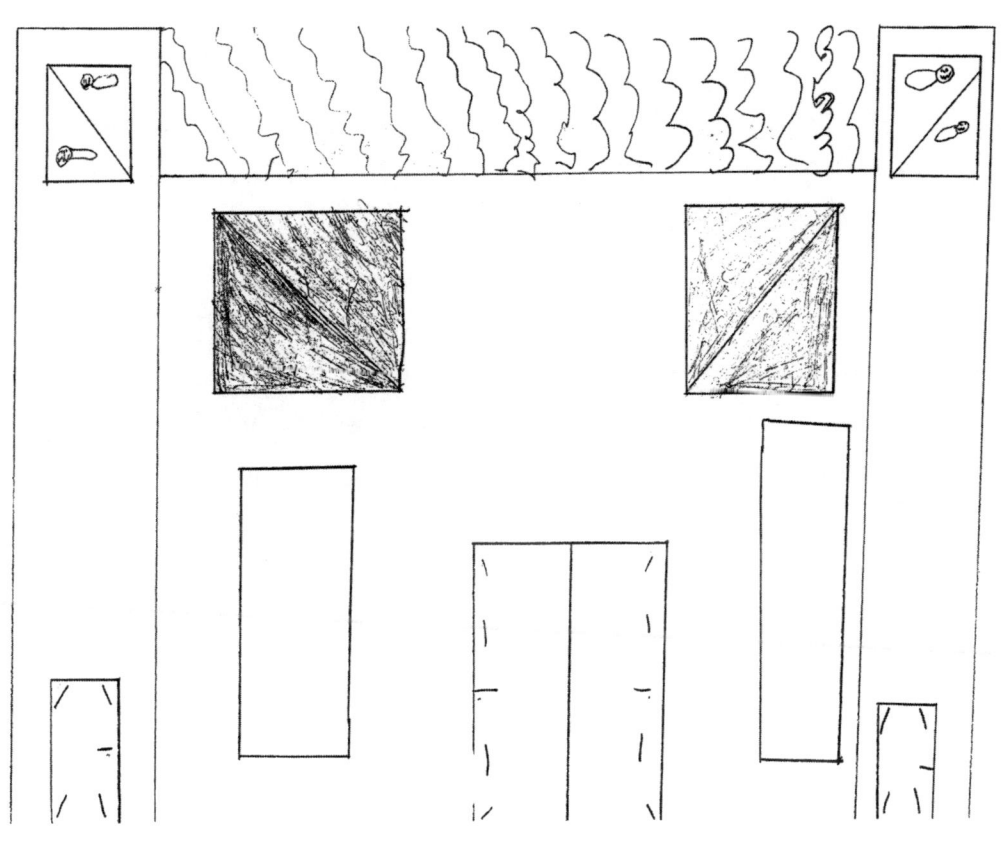

Bella Leong-Smith

The immense house towered over the trees. Leaning in its frame was a muddy, dilapidated door with a rusted doorknob. The grounds were almost extinct, taken of life, unless you were counting the crows.

Inside the immense, mysterious house there was no furniture apart from a single box. Like an abandoned dog, the building seemed to pine for company. That is, if you were staying. For a terror which has haunted this house for a millennia has awakened! And it feeds!

Slowly, I crept up the eerily silent steps. Despite my will to leave, the house drew me towards it, like bait for a tiger. Gigantic windows, twice the size of a fully grown man, were smashed and glass littered the staircase.

I gingerly pushed the door. To my surprise, and luck, or what I thought was, the door opened…

There was a ferocious scream and a straggly haired young woman with green skin came running at me.

Bella Leong-Smith

She was some sort of cross between a banshee and a fire breathing dragon. A bansheathing? Or a banshire? When I heard that scream, one way or another I knew I had to die. Tripping, I let out a scream myself. All of a sudden I thought, 'I'm going to die here,' and I knew I must flee.

Terror froze my body. Yes, I was out of the house, but…the path was totally flooded. There was no way home. I was trapped! The sun had just said goodbye. At the age of ten I had ignored the scout motto – 'Be prepared.' I had come empty handed and I was about to regret it!

Emily Brook

The light flickered then disappeared. I stood up and looked around. 'Where am I?' I thought. The deafening silence was unbearable. Anything to break it would be fine. Except for what I heard. A ghostly scream echoed in the valley and shook the crumbling rock castle. All the trees surrounding it and the stiff iron gates.

Slowly, I looked around for an escape. I saw a trap door. But then a voice whispered in my ear, 'Go into the house. Step straight in.'

It was so beautiful that I went, in a trance, until I got to the gate.

Creaking open it edged forwards until it made a tremendous CRASH! And I was pulled forth once again. Quickly I turned to leave but I was paralysed with fear. Something edged me into the ruins and that was when I saw the figure. I blinked. It disappeared. Running as fast as I could I followed it into a ginormous room. Looking up I realised the danger I was in. The roof collapsed so I rolled. I rolled into a new room.

The room had a set of cobweb covered stairs on one side. The figure floated up them. I felt a sudden urge to follow. As I stepped up onto the first step it creaked extremely loudly. I figured out that if I went up quickly it wouldn't be so scary. So I ran. It was all going fine until suddenly, I fell straight through the step.

I grasped at the remains, holding on for dear life. The remains fell. They broke off in my hands. So I jumped and I landed on the previous step. I didn't dare speak. I just jumped over the disaster step and carried on.

Once I arrived at the top there was something mysterious going on. I could feel it. As I wandered around the abandoned halls and corridors nothing prepared me for what happened next. A deafening cackle surrounded me, then…the entire house collapsed. And so did I. I am a spirit now!

Jake Ferguson

I wanted to go to the house as the last rays of light were fading to darkness. The house was in sight. It felt like it was pulling me in when I saw strange figures around the house. I blinked and they were gone.

The house was by the sea. It had thousands of cobwebs and a bit of ivy dangling here and there. I got to the house and slowly opened the door. Inside the house I froze to look around. Carefully and slowly I walked up the stairs and I saw a figure down a long hallway.

I walked to the kitchen and everything was broken. I walked to a different room. It was the scariest of all the bedrooms. A bed was there but nothing else. Just a bed. I froze. A strange figure walked in then disappeared. I froze in terror. Mysteriously, the door shut tight. I could not move.

I got my strength back and carried on to go to the next room. It was the living room with a couch cut in half and a burnt fireplace. The whole carpet was burned and there was still a fire where the last bit of rug and carpet was burning.

Jake Ferguson

Just then a different figure appeared. It looked like a dog or a cat, maybe. But before I could see it properly it disappeared. It seemed like I was in a haunted house! I started to imagine the people that had lived here long ago. I tried to find the exit. One hour of searching and I didn't find it. Two hours later I found a staircase but it was the wrong one but I still looked though.

Harlie Clayworth

I had been dreaming of going to the house on the island ever since my grandmother told me about it.

'No one has ever been there before,' she whispered.

Today I was trembling and spluttering not wanting to go. Finally, the hour came. I could not wait to get this over with.

At the gates of the house I jumped at everything, even a seagull! Blinking at the house I saw a figure. They were tall and slim and wore a pointy hat. Just like a witch! I needed another look just to make sure there was someone there. But no one was there.

'I am imagining stuff!' I told myself.

All I could do was walk in. So I walked over to the tall black case in the middle of a dull yellow garden full of nettles and weeds ready to grab my feet. When I was past all the nettles I was trembling. I pushed the door with my shaky hand and then… 'Creeeaaak!' the door opened and I almost froze at the sight of the misty brown stairs curving around the edges of the long hall. As I got closer I got slower. Shaking cobwebs off the stairs I stumbled up trying not to make a sound.

Each stair was like a hurdle. They were so tall and they were ten feet wide. Finally, I was up the stairs and I went into a large room with a flying bat. It had a brick and wood floor.

I suddenly felt a strong wind blowing froth the salty sea. A thought came to me, 'Will I get home before a storm starts?' I started weeping and I sat at a table marked: Potions of Poison! Intruder do not touch! I wanted to scream and shout but I didn't dare. For all I knew was that I was not safe in the house. A noise from outside made me shiver…

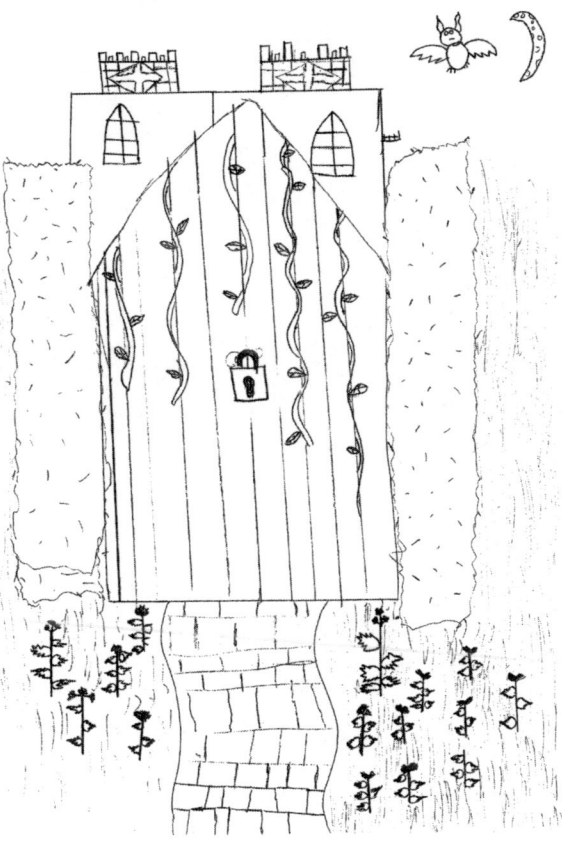

189

Tamlin Scott

I was slowly approaching a house I had been visiting for many years. Approaching the gates I had felt the saltiness of the old gates from when the tides came in over many years. I slowly approached the front garden of the house.

Tamlin Scott

With a shiver down my spine, I looked up with a glance and saw a gloomy figure in the window at the top of the peak of the mansion. Suddenly, the gloomy figure disappeared in a flash like a ghost.

I slowly stepped up the stairs. I kept seeing gloomy figures and a dog and a lot of tigers around upstairs. Then I suddenly froze with ice up my spine. The ghostly figures glanced at me and I glanced at them. Then suddenly, they disappeared in a flash.

I slowly walked upstairs and thought to myself, 'Is this real, or is this just a dream?' I slowly crept to the master bedroom, got out my torch, looked in the room and saw two skeletons on the big bed holding hands like a married couple.

Adam Young

I've always been excited to come here, for days and days. So I did all by myself. I was here now so I unpacked and went to see my neighbours but there was only my house and the house next door. I went around to them and rang the door bell. There was no answer but I heard a ghost noise. I quickly ran home and got a drink.

It was a day later that I thought I needed to get out of here. I got all my stuff and got up to the gates but the ghost shut them and made them really tall. I ran into the house and I heard some crying from a ghost in my bedroom.

I went in and the ghost said, 'No don't hurt me!'

'I won't. What is your name?' I said.

'Spencer,' said Spencer the ghost.

Year 6

HATCHET

I'm running. Running away as fast as I can. There's no chance to catch my breath. If I stop then he'll get me. I don't even know who he is. But I know I have to keep going.

I trip over a twig, badly scratching my knee so that it rips right through my trousers and tears my skin. I lie there for a moment, almost motionless, clutching my aching knee but savouring my brief moment of rest. I have to keep going I keep telling myself. Get up now! I have to keep going.

The fall gave me a chance to catch my breath but my knee is still bleeding. My heart is pounding inside my chest, fit to burst from it at any moment and my knee aches more with every step I take. I have to keep going.

I lost precious time when I fell, despite that he is only stumbling in a zombie-like fashion. I have to keep going! I HAVE to keep going!

Oh no! A dead end! I have to turn back but there's no chance of that now. I'm rooted to the ground like the trees which surround me. I'm filled with uncontrollable fear. I listen to their whispers – some sound sympathetic like they are trying to help me, others seem to cheer on the man who pursues me. Then they all begin to chant, 'We can't save the girl!' once again, 'The man you see before you is Hatchet. Hatchet. Hatchet takes a life again.'

He was closer than ever now. I could smell his rotting breath, taste his musty evil scent on the tip of my tongue and just make out his distorted face in the ever darkening gloom.

'Who – wh – who are you?' I staggered trying to find the right words and say them as calmly and confidently as possible.

'The name's Hatchet,' he mumbled with just the confidence and calmness I had aimed for.

He had a mild cockney tone, where as my voice is an odd

mix of mancunian and non-cockney. (I'm not quite sure what you would call it – perhaps Londonish.) He began to roar with evil laughter.

The trees were louder than ever now, constantly repeating, 'Hatchet, Hatchet, Hatchet,' over and over again in their child like moaning voices. He raised something high above his head and I just made out a glint of metal before he swung the thing down and I screamed in pure terror.

Silence.

I sat up in my bed, taking a sharp breath. A lightning bolt struck outside as a storm raged uncontrollably. I looked over at my alarm clock. It turned 02:16 the moment I laid eyes on it. The exact same time as last night and the night before that. My dreams were always the same now, they were always about him. My worst nightmare.

Suddenly, Meg, my older cousin, came rushing into my room. 'That was quite a scream you let out there!' she exclaimed, a look of certain concern on her face. 'You okay little cuz?'

I explained it all to her and she listened to every word before tucking me up and hopping into bed with me to sing me a lullaby. I know it's babyish right! But it worked a treat!

When I woke up it was morning. My morning went by pretty normally, except for at morning break there was a shady looking man hiding behind the trees by the gate. I felt as if he was watching me. His gaze burned me and made me feel hot and sweaty all over. He was still there at lunch, but this time he was holding something. I couldn't make it out in the shade from the old sycamore, but I didn't like the look of it.

As I left school, I noticed that the man wasn't there anymore. I began on my way home as though a great weight had been lifted off my shoulders. I was the calmest I'd been in weeks! But as I passed the corner shop I noticed a man who appeared to have been following me. He had an eerie feel about him so I decided to walk a bit faster…and a little bit faster…and a little bit faster still until I was running.

He was still behind me! It was getting very dark now and the winter air nipped and slapped my face and hands as I ran. I tried to slip into the woods while he wasn't looking but it didn't work.

I'm running. Running away as fast as I can. There's no chance to catch my breath. If I stop then he'll get me. I don't even know who he is. But I know I have to keep going.

It's all happening…

By Evie Brook

JACOB'S GONNA GET YOU!

One night, after watching a movie called, Jacob's Gonna Get You, the Simpson family were worried. They all had nightmares about who Jacob was and what he wanted them for.

The next morning they found out why…They needn't have worried because Jacob wanted to find them to let them know that they had won a family trip, all expenses paid to the farm.

By Jacob Santon

SHIPWRECKED

As Alex woke up she thought so hard about her mum and how she didn't say goodbye. See Alex was an average eleven year old girl. She had a big brother called Jim, he was thirteen and very lazy.

Alex, Jim and their mum Clare, had been on a ship to Jamaica when the sea started to get rough and, well, before they knew it people started to abandon ship. Luckily, Alex got a small rowing boat and sailed ashore. The others weren't so lucky. Only Alex survived, or so she thought...

After a while, Alex decided to go for a little stroll into the jungle. As she got further in she stopped. 'Cough.' Alex almost jumped out of her skin! Looking around she spotted a boy laid on the rocks. He stretched his bony arms and legs and slumped back down on the rocks, not even noticing Alex. But before he even had a chance to breathe, Alex hugged him as tight as she could. It was Jim! After they had finished hugging they both went back to go to sleep.

Stretching in the summer sun Alex and Jim woke up from a good night's sleep. As Alex leaped up to her feet she ran towards the deep blue sea. A couple of seconds later she was rowing her way to shore. 'Come on, get in.' she cried, as she sat in the boat. Jim hopped in and they sailed home.

By Maia Ogunsola

NIGHTMARES

Hi, my name is Maria. I am ten years old. I have an older brother and sister. They are called Zac and Donna. My mum and dad are called Steven and Karen.

'Maria! Donna! Zac! Time for school!' Dad called from the very bottom of the solid brown stairs.

I hate school with a capital H, because people are really mean, plus the work is too hard. Donna is very clever, I don't know about Zac though. My parents always tell me that if I don't do well at school I won't have much money, so when I have kids, if I do, they won't be healthy.

When I get to school I was very late, again. I just blamed it on the traffic. 'Maria!' screeched Miss Bailey from down the hall, 'This is the third time being late. Go and see the Head Teacher to explain what you have done!'

I don't mind going to see the Head Teacher.

'Why are you here this time?' Mrs Partner growled as she opened her old, creaky door.

'Because it's the third time being late,' I told her in a proud voice.

All lunchtime I had to stay in the classroom and help – boring!

Once I got home my mum and dad were upstairs packing

bags. I didn't know what for.

'Hi, are we going on holiday?' announced Maria, 'I love holidays!'

'Sorry, but no. We're moving house.'

I hate moving house. I've just made new friends but I will just be alright with it.

'Oh! Why didn't you tell me?' I was a bit confused.

'It was a surprise.'

The next day when Maria went to school she had to break the news to people. 'I'm leaving on Friday!' At home-time, I thought that my mum would pick me up, but she didn't, she was too busy packing.

'How was your day at school?' my mum asked as I walked through the door.

'Horrible!'

'Never mind. We are going to order tea tonight.'

By Chloe Brannon

HEROBRINE AND THE APOCALYPSE!

As the sun peered through the red see-through curtains, my alarm played the jolly theme song of Sponge Bob. 'Ahh!' I yawned as I leaped out of bed.

Step by step I hurried to the recently cleaned bathroom to brush my teeth. Surprisingly, I heard a loud knock at my door and I wondered who it could be. As I opened the door I felt that something bad was happening.

'Sir, please can you barricade your doors and windows and make sure you don't go outside. Once you've done that turn on your TV and switch to Channel 4 news immediately,' the policeman commanded as he wrote something down in his note pad, 'It's so they don't getchya!'

'Who? When?' I questioned desperately.

There was no reply. I was scared but more confused. At the speed of light I shut the front door and quickly ran upstairs and turned on the TV to Channel 4 news, only to see...

It was an apocalypse! But this wasn't any ordinary apocalypse, it was filled with weird creatures. They had names such as: Creepers; something that follows you around and self destructs when it gets within range leaving you badly injured. A skeleton; it carries unlimited arrows. It also has nothing else apart from bones. A zombie; they usually appear in big groups and they eat your brains! A slime; a big, green blob that swallows you up. If you kill a big one it will turn into four little ones. An Enderman; a strange creature that has the ability to teleport and move big objects with its ridiculously long arms. Finally, we have Herobrine, he is the ruler of the creatures and beside him his huge pet Enderdragon called Killer.

Only the bravest of people could defeat them all and I, Steve, was one of them. So I gathered together my army and set off to beat Herobrine!

What we needed was simple but hard to get. We needed poisonous potions to make them weak; strength

potions to make us even stronger and diamond armour and a sword. We also needed to enchant our gear to make us even stronger.

HEROBRINE AND THE APOCALYPSE!

We were going to win this and nothing could stop us. One by one we headed outside and we tried our best to kill the creatures. Eventually, we were at the end. We were all face to face with Herobrine, the devil in this world.

'Wait!' shouted a familiar voice.

'Notch!' we all shouted, 'you've come to help us!'

We were all ready. We threw our poisonous potions and drank our strength potions. It was a tough fight but we did it.

'Whooohooo!' we all shouted with delight, 'We did it!'

The next day I woke up and I heard a knock at my door. 'Steve! Get up now. You're going to be late for school!' shouted my mum.

WOW! It was all just a dream!

By Joe Dickson

THE POSSESSED DOLL

1771 was the year when a family of four moved into a three story house. The family had a mother, a father and two daughters, Rosie and Mary. Rosie was the youngest.

When Rosie went to her room, she found a white doll with a blue and red skirt, a purple jumper, blonde hair, a huge scar across its face, but Rosie didn't mind.

During their first night in the dark, damp house, a gust of wind came into Rosie's room and straight into the doll. The doll got out of the bed that it was in and walked slowly downstairs. Bang! A loud noise exploded and all the family rushed downstairs and went into the living room.

The doll locked them in. It used her evil magic and made everything in the room jump up and spin in a circle until they reached death. Then, she hid the bodies in the shed next to the house.

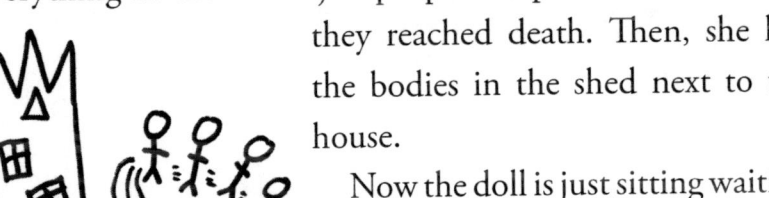

Now the doll is just sitting waiting for the next family to arrive…

By Holly Christie Harwood

WHAT A DREAM!

One very fine but mild night, a young girl, called Sofia, was kissing her mother goodnight when suddenly the lightness turned into darkness. It was that dark that after a couple of very long minutes Sofia was in a deep sleep.

Eventually, Sofia was having a dream. This strange dream was about a superhero that was called Bob the Bear. This was strange because you can't really imagine a bear who saved the world, can you?

Bob's fantastic job was to fly around houses and help people who were in trouble. If the children who Bob helped were kind and considerate, they would receive a scrumptious treat! Bob is the kindest superhero in the world!

That was until one day a horrible figure called Evil Mack, who was very evil, destroyed Bob the Bear and tried to stop him being so fantastic! Everyone in the village was devastated when

they heard that Bob had gone missing! No one knew where Bob had gone! So people started getting upset and more and more people were getting into trouble. With no one to help the whole of the village was unhappy.

As Evil Mack was being so evil, Super Bob went onto Bearbook – another version of Facebook – and asked his friends to: A. Come and rescue him and B. To get rid of Evil Mack!

As Bob's friends were about to come and rescue Bob, Sofia woke up. It was already morning so that was good that she didn't finish the dream in the middle of the night! Sofia sighed as she was about to come to the good bit of the dream. Time flies when you're having fun!

By Rosanna Main

ROSIE'S HOLIDAY

The gold bright sun gleamed right through the light weight curtains, but Rosie was in one of her exciting dreams again. She didn't want to wake up, she was too busy dreaming about going on a holiday.

Rosie, her mum and her dad were in their big black car on their way to the airport. They had all their suitcases in the boot. Rosie was excited because it was her first time going on a plane. Rosie's mum and dad had already been on a holiday before.

When she got to the airport, she couldn't believe what was happening. She was so happy and excited. This would be the first time she'd ever been abroad. It was nearly time for her to get her suitcases, when she would be getting on the plane.

She was in line to show her passport. When she had shown her passport she tiptoed onto the creaky floorboards of the plane. She could see row after row seats all next to each other. Rosie's mum and dad sat down right in the middle, so Rosie followed them. Rosie sat down comfortably and put her head back against the rest as she started falling to sleep.

After two long hours, Rosie woke up. She grabbed all her things, then they got off the plane. There were lots of coaches waiting there. Rosie and her mum and dad got on their coach. It took forty minutes until she got to her hotel. After she did, they parked outside a big, tall, white hotel. They all stepped off the coach and walked through the automatic doors.

Rosie and her family went into the lift to go up to their apartment with their suitcases. When they came out of the lift they got their key and opened the door and walked into their massive apartment. Rosie got the smallest room, but she wasn't bothered.

She was looking around in the rooms. She really liked her room. Rosie opened a big door that led to the balcony and there were other people sat down on their balconies too.

That's when she heard her mum shout, 'Wake up!' Rosie yawned and stretched and the holiday dream was now finished. Rosie wished that the dream would come true some day.

By Kayleigh Donnelly

TITANIC

Dear Rose,

I am writing to you to tell you about the thrilling but scary experience I had on the grandest ship ever built in the world, the Titanic.

A long time ago in 1912, I experienced a thrilling ride on the Titanic. The huge ship set sail from Ireland hoping to reach New York in a record breaking time.

My family and I boarded the ship whilst the drive drove our new top of the range motorcar onto the ship.

As I walked through the grand ship upper deck, I was shocked to see lots of famous and well connected people in the first class lounge.

As time went on, the ship set sail and I settled down into my beautiful cabin which was decorated with the finest cloths and silks. It really was luxurious!

I spent my days walking the deck with my new friends from Southampton and taking in the sea air. Tea was served in the finest china I had ever seen. We were really treated like royalty.

My life changed from living my dream in the first class decks, to living my worst nightmare. As a few days passed by it was the 15th of April, 1912 when the great disaster happened.

At 9:30pm, my family and I were having a glass of wine on the deck, when all of a sudden the ship crashed into a solid iceberg. This made a huge hole in the hull of the ship which caused a lot of things to go wrong.

The captain said that we only had an hour to get everyone off this boat before it sank. Everyone was in a rush trying to get a boat to save themselves. Ladies and children had to go first. It was time for this ship to go down into the ocean.

By Megan Routh

VICTORIAN TIMES

I wonder what it would have been like in 1837? When the wicked teachers had to do the terrible whipping and all the children never had any fun. Only wearing grey clothes. If I was in that place I would try to escape. I would never want to stay in Victorian times.

I wonder what it would have been like in 1837? Eating our lunch in the gigantic dinner halls. Even if they were allowed to speak, I bet the children were absolutely terrified. I would hate to be in the classroom with the teacher. She could just whip you even if you said one single thing. I would never want to stay in Victorian Times.

I wonder what it would have been like in 1837? They had to write on mini chalk boards on their little desk. Imagine that if you got a question wrong, you would probably get whipped. I would never want to stay in Victorian times.

I wonder what it would have been like in 1837? On the bare streets, some poor then some rich. Those people wearing flouncy dresses. I would never want to stay in Victorian times.

I wonder what it would have been like in 1837? No fun now. I would not fit in there – not at all! There will just be children all miserable just sat in the classroom, quiet as can be. I would never want to stay in Victorian times.

I wonder what it would be like in 1837? Would they have nice food? Or would it just be disgusting? I would really never want to stay in Victorian times.

I wonder what it would be like in 1837? Would they have nice teachers or would they just be cruel? I would really hate to experience Victorian times.

By Samantha Bradshaw

MY BIRTHDAY HORROR

Waking up at 7:30am, I'll never do that again! It's my birthday! Hurray! I wish I didn't live here. By the time I reached the living room, my motionless parents woke up. They shouted, 'Get us a cup of coffee, Alex.'

I mean, come on! Can't she move? So I decided to say, 'No! Make the coffee yourself!'

After that I pounced on the sofa like a cat. Should I go upstairs to see what my brother and sister are wrestling about? Nah, its probably something pointless.

I set off to school, but it seems like my parents don't even notice. 'Oh well,' I sighed, slamming the door shut.

'Is she gone yet?' my parents whispered as they peered through the curtains.

The school playground was deserted, it also reeked of garbage. This place is a dump. Then Charlie came round the corner looking stressed, as always! She yanked me hard into our tunnel and she whispered, 'Don't freak out and don't tell anyone, but I'm an angel.'

I glared at her gob-smacked.

216

'Right, let's go or we're going to be late for our concert.'

My beady eyes stared at her, 'Come on she's kidding, right?

Then my beady eyes were concentrating on something else. Max and Ellie, as usual were squabbling their way into school. Charlie was going to flash us out when Ellie came with us, so looks like were taking her with us.

We turned up in this Minecraft shop. The door was locked but the shopkeeper was still in. Charlie's angel magic was working and there's no WiFi, what kind of stupid shop doesn't have WiFi!?

The shop keeper crept towards us. We tiptoed backwards. Ellie hid behind me, she snuggled tight. I could tell she was terrified. Suddenly, out of nowhere these people came towards us like zombies.

I saw a lifeless gun on the tiled floor. I saw a bunch of zombies, I quickly grabbed the gun. I had the target in sight. I closed my eyes and pulled the trigger…BANG! I dared not look but when I did Charlie looked at me her mouth wide open. I didn't know why until I saw Ellie there. She looked like a lifeless doll. I knew then there was no way I was going to cope without her. She was dead…

We didn't know what to do. We sobbed and sobbed. We are never going home even if it is my birthday!

By Sophie Gregson

A NIGHTMARE FROM THE FUTURE

I ran and ran, not daring to look back at the mob of wraiths, seven foot tall ghosts with burning skin, clad in coal black rags, that were pursuing me. It felt like I'd been running for hours for my muscles burned and my throat, now and again, closed up. The wraiths never seemed to tire.

Suddenly, I was falling ever downward and then…Splash! I tried to breath but I couldn't because there was water all around me and that's when I realised my heavy boots were forcing me to sink! With that I started to fumble with my laces in a desperate attempt to save myself.

Once one was off, I started to slowly rise upwards. But I feared it was too late because I was feeling very light in the head. Finally, when I thought I was just about to go into unconsciousness. I broke the surface of the water. Immediately, I realised I was in the middle of the ocean because all I could see was water and more water.

After recovering form my near death experience, I took the other boot off which helped me to float. Squinting in the afternoon sun I looked for any sign of help.

Finally, after what seemed like an eternity, I saw a little fishing boat on the horizon. When it got nearer I started to wave and shout trying to get the captain's attention. Luckily, the captain was nice and let me aboard.

When I got home to two relieved parents, I was bombarded by questions from the press. But now everything is back to normal again. Or so I thought...

By Thomas Rigby

BURT THE BLACK CREATURE

One creepy, dark night it was 3am and Joe saw a scary, black looking creature with glowing red eyes, but he didn't know because it was dark, darker than ever.

Joe only woke up because he heard a screeching, strange noise from the kitchen downstairs. So he tiptoed downstairs without making a sound to see what it was, but there was nothing there.

Joe went back upstairs to bed to sleep because it was a school night. He got back to sleep until another strange noise occurred, so he went downstairs once more to see what it was.

The black creature showed itself and he told Joe that he wasn't here to hurt anybody, he was just there for food and that his name was Burt.

'Oh, here's some food,'

said Joe, as he buttered the bread.

Burt stuffed his face until there was nothing in the house.

When mum and dad woke up they went mad at Joe for losing their house.

'It wasn't me. It was Burt!' Joe cried.

'Who's Burt?' asked mum with her hands on her hips.

'A black creature who has been in the wild for ages and he was hungry.'

'Okay, we believe you,' replied Dad, whilst he tentatively looked out of the kitchen window. 'Will Burt be coming back?'

By Corban Calvert

AMY MEETS
THE QUEEN

'For the seventh hundredth time Amy, get up!' screamed mum, as she made her first cup of tea. Amy leapt out of her bed quickly and happily. Amy knew she had a long tiring day ahead of her. She was going to London!

'What do you want for breakfast?' asked mum, walking towards the bottom of the stairs.

'Toast,' bellowed Amy in reply, throwing on her crumpled school uniform.

'When you've done that come down and get your breakfast.'

Amy strolled down the stairs pulling her jumper over her head.

'When you've finished your breakfast go and brush your teeth, brush your hair and wash your face.'

When breakfast was finished, mum and Amy collected their bags and walked towards the front door. After a short drive they arrived at the local train station. There were chattering businessmen drinking strong coffee and tourists checking the various timetables. Then children filed onto the waiting train. They got to sit next to whoever they wanted.

On the way, Amy fell asleep.

The class led my Mrs Tee, navigated their way through the busy city via tube, ferry and bus, finally reaching their destination – the amazing Buckingham Palace.

It was a breath taking sight.

'Have you got the letter Mrs Tee?' asked Amy, pushing her way to the front of the line. 'We need it to get it in.'

'Of course Amy, would you like to hand it to the guard?' asked Mrs Tee.

By Megan Mackintosh-Green

A Scary Owl

One horrible windy morning, I was laid in my bed with nothing to do. As I'm snuggled up in my warm duvet, I heard something strange and also saw something fluffy, red eyed and freaky. Then I ran to my mum but she wasn't there. I thought, 'No, noooo, no! This can't be happening. That owl has eaten her!' I jumped in my bed with fear and cried myself to sleep.

As soon as I opened my eyes the next day, I sensed something straight away that something wasn't right. I ran to my mum downstairs and told her about the dreadful night I had.

'Don't be silly you are fine. Don't worry,' she replied.

I didn't feel very well. I don't like being ill I thought. I went for a lie down. I heard a twit twoo. I didn't dare move.

I looked out of my window and it was there; big red eyes and a scary face looking at me. I froze for a second, I screamed at the top of my voice but nobody seamed to hear. I banged and banged on the window to get it away but it wouldn't have non of it.

I started to cry. Mum sat next to me and said, 'Codie, it's absolutely fine. You just had a little nightmare.'

'A little nightmare!' I replied.

By Codie Chapman

DIRT 9#

Today is a hot sunny Saturday in June. Josh was dirt biking for the bikes world championship contest. That day finally came around but the bad thing was that it was a very long journey to Manchester where the championship was being held.

After that we unloaded the truck and put on my dirt biking shirt and my helmet. Then I practiced so hard that sweat was dripping down my face. Dirt was now up, doing 360 backwards spins.

Next day was the quarter final and Dirt was in it. Dirt did the twist 1000 and loads of air time. The announcer called for break time. For his lunch he got the double cheese burger with an extra large fanta. Then his manager A.K.A. His Dad spoke to him. But it was nice and cool which made him ready for the next round.

At last the final round came and it was him against his rival. It was Mud Man vs Dirt. Mud Man went first and did the 360 backwards spin twist with no air time. Dirt went last and did his signature move the Dirt 9 and he won! The crowd went wild. 'Yeeehaaa!'

Who was Dirt...

By Josh Sloan-Lewis

MY
FOOTBALL DREAM

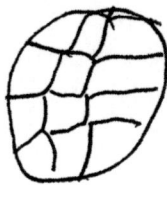

Hi, Jack here, and I'm going to write a story about my dream.

My dream is to become a legend at Everton Football Club (E.F.C.) Personally, I would love it to walk to the shop and find a fan that wanted my autograph or to see a fan with an Everton shirt on with Birchy on the back of it. Birchy is my nickname. That would be rated 'A' for awesome!

Since I have heard about the legend, Duncan Ferguson, he has been my hero. Although he was a bit tough, he was a great football player. The thing that would make the icing on the cake is being made captain of Everton and winning the F.A. Cup.

But there are some horrible nightmares about playing

football…

As I was saying you can get injured and this is a nightmare because you could be playing really good and then you could be injured and you never start again. Or, you could just play really good one season and play awful for the next.

This is a true story. An Everton player called Bryan Oviedo was playing in a F.A. Cup match and one of his team mates, Gareth Barry, broke Bryan's leg. It was a horrible time for Bryan because this happened in January 2014, and he is still injured. It is so annoying for us Everton fans because he was having a superb season.

This is my dream…

By Jack Birch

DREAM
AND
NIGHTMARE

One day on Friday the 13th of December, Lucy, Megan, Ami and Milly all went to town. Then they saw a fluffy unicorn sliding on a rainbow in the shop window. Ami then had a daydream about sliding down and down the rainbow with the fluffy unicorn.

The next minute a boy called Joe fell into her from having a race with his friend pulling her out of her daydream.

'Oh I am so sorry!' gasped Joe, as he was racing his friend to the toy shop.

'It's okay Joe,' replied Ami, as she carried on staring in the shop window.

Then Milly had a nightmare instead of a dream. It was about a scary person who was wearing a black hoodie and following her everywhere she goes. So she was scared.

The next time Megan had a dream about seeing her favourite bands which were Little Mix and One Direction and get a picture with all of them and get an autograph of Niall Horan.

Lucy had a dream about seeing Katy Perry and meeting Liam Payne out of One Direction and going to high school with her friends.

The last thing of the day, they all went to Megan's house and had pizza for tea. Then they had a big sleepover and had a big pillow fight.

'I wonder what dream or nightmare we well have next time at the sleepover?' whispered all of them in a creepy voice.

By Tia Leak

WORLD WAR THREE: A TRAGIC TALE

Dear Diary,

I wish I had never joined the army. I wish I never signed the contract. I wish today never happened at all. Today was horrendous. I will start the story at our base camp in Moscow.

I was rudely awakened by my friend, Saffron. She was shouting at me for not getting up even though it was only 6:30am. This was the usual time for me to rise from my slumber. Then I told her that I was awake and she didn't need to deafen me anymore. After that she swiftly walked away to leave me to get ready for the long day ahead.

Once we were all ready we jumped into the black, newly washed Range Rover, and set off to the uncharted streets of Moscow in search of bombs or bomb factories. We had been driving round the streets for hours when Evie, our co-worker friend, spotted a gigantic warehouse, which looked suspiciously like it stored bombs. Saffron volunteered to go first.

'Wait Saffron!' I shouted.

She turned around.

'It could be a trap so be careful,' I warned.

She nodded.

After five minutes we got worried and suddenly we heard

a scream followed by an explosion.

'SAFFRON!' I screamed as we ran into the warehouse to find a dead body on the floor.

R.I.P. Saffron Brownson. In a week I am attending her funeral but for now give me hope.

Your faithful friend, Toni

By Abbey Atkin

R.I.P Saffron
Brownson

I'm Not Dead!

I was standing there in a pitch black room with only a candle for a light. I could hear my family crying and sad music playing. As I shuffled about I called out to see if anyone was there but unfortunately I was on my own. Suddenly, I heard a vicar saying sad sympathy prayers in an upset voice.

Then from the corner of my eye, I spotted an enormous mahogany door that had a crack of dim light coming from it. As I walked towards the door the prayers got louder and so did the crying.

With a deep breath I opened the door and to my surprise it led to the back of a church and sitting in the church was all my family and friends.

They were all staring at a picture of me next to a rosewood coffin.

'What's all of this?' I yelled as if I had been part of a nasty joke.

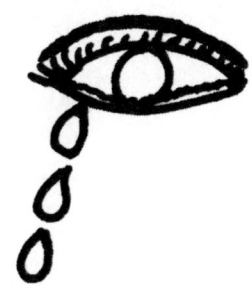

'Oh my!' my mum sobbed.

I can still hear her sweet voice now. Then I realised I was at my own funeral.

How can I be dead? I thought to myself. The last thing I could remember was that I was on my way home from high school with my friends, Kayleigh and Sammy, when BAM! Everything went black!

A few seconds later I heard a familiar voice. 'Everything will be okay,' it said.

'GRANDAD,' I bellowed.

But as I went to give him a hug he started to fade and disappear but before he had fully gone he gave me a golden cross necklace in my hand. It had a beautiful glittering ruby in the middle.

As I woke up from my dream, totally clueless about what had happened, I found the necklace on my neck and that I was in a hospital bed. I will never forget that about my grandad.

By Ruby Seaton

THE MIRACLE

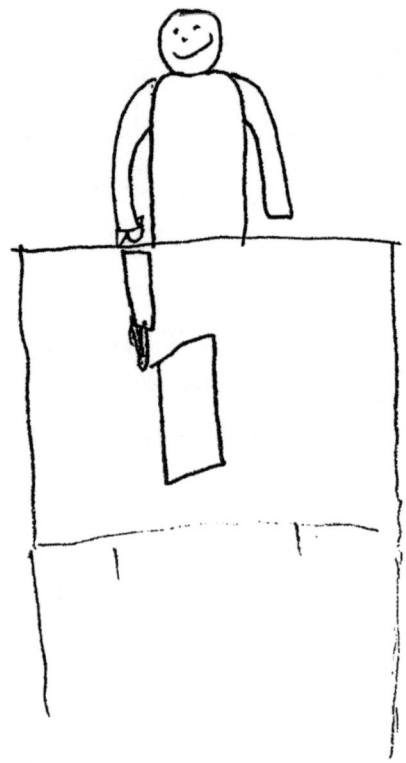

I woke up, the sun beaming and hitting me in the face. Today was the last day of SATS – a day of boring tests which I really couldn't be bothered to do. Mum, who was shouting for me to go to school, put her woolly coat on and rushed Bobby to nursery.

Later, I arrived at school. My first test was Level 6 maths, Paper 1, with no calculator. My first out of two today. Looking apprehensive, Miss Stephenson gave me a glimpse as if to say come on do your best. We had one last look at the wall then we walked in ready to nail this test.

As we started the test I really couldn't be bothered but to get a good mark I had to do my best to get a level 6. I was halfway through the test and I'd nearly finished. It felt extremely easy – the first test always does. Question after question I worked out the answers until finally the test was finished.

The test had finished and we got to go out for a bit of fresh air before we attempted the second test. As usual Jacob talked about how good he was on the X-Box.

Ten minutes later…

We had just started the second test. It was a lot harder than the first. It had a lot of questions on co-ordinates and I find them really tricky. Me! Who was getting really bored, was on question six half way through the test. Before I knew it I had ten minutes left – no time whatsoever and when it's like that I feel pressure. Five minutes left, I'd finished and I could leave early but now I have to wait for the results…

8th July 2014. The results, 'I GOT A LEVEL 6!'

By Luke Sprules

WHAT A NIGHTMARE!

It was a cold, stormy night, the wind was howling, it was thundering and lightning, everyone was in bed. But there was this one little girl having the worst nightmare of her life.

'AAHHR!' screamed Hannah as she awoke from her terrifying nightmare. Her parents raced into the untidy bedroom.

'Hannah!' her dad hesitated, 'Are you all right?'

At this point Hannah was crying and couldn't get her words out.

'Sweetie, it was just a nightmare,' her mum sighed as she calmed her daughter down, 'tell me what happened,' Mum whispered softly.

'Well,' sobbed Hannah, 'this is how it all began…'

'Hey guys! Ready for a night of fun?' questioned Hannah.

'Yeah!' cried Tommy. Tommy had just collected his and Hannah's friends, Jake, Alice and Mary-Jo, and they were having a sleepover at Hannah and Tommy's grandad's farm.

It was twelve o'clock and everyone was in bed.

TIP-TOE-TIP-TOE-TIP-TOE-TIP-TOE!

'Hey does anyone hear that noise?' whispered Mary-Jo.

Everyone was now awake and looked underneath the door of the barn they were sleeping in, but of course Hannah and

Tommy's mum were sleeping in the barn next door to them.

'I think... Hey does anyone see a shadow!' cried Alice as she pointed to the tree in the corner of the deserted farm.

'Yeah, you can just make out the phantom cloak it's wearing,' Jake pointed out.

'It's going into mum's barn...!' yelled Hannah.

'AAAHHHRRR!' came a scream from the other barn.

'MUM!' Shouted Tommy and Hannah and they ran into the barn their mum was in. But it was too late, their mum... was dead...

'Hannah it is all right, I'm right here, I would never leave you,' Mum promised.

'I told you not to eat that cheese before bed, now go to sleep honey.'

'Ok Mum,' Hannah replied as she snuggled up to her teddy bear.

What Hannah did not realise, was that her entire life was about to be flipped upside down...

By Lucy Wenlock

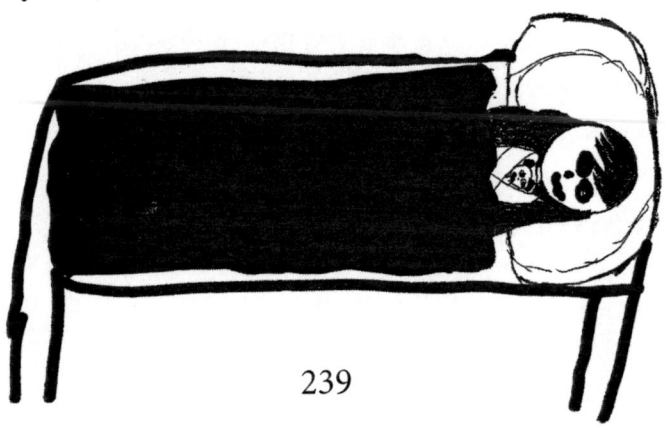

THE SKELETON BOY

It was a cold and windy night in Mistik Manor and Thomas Rawlinson was in bed waiting for the big race, the Tour de France. He rode for team sky.

In the morning he got into his costume that made him look like a human and that is because he is a skeleton! He went downstairs and had some toast. Then he went into the shed where he kept his bikes. He got his best bike to check it was ready. It was and it was a Pinardlo – the best bike in the world.

When he got there, he lined up on the starting line and set off. But halfway there he crashed into the back of a truck. Thomas' costume came off! Everyone watching gasped. He went past everyone and across the line in first place and he became the most popular person in the world.

By Thomas Michael Bates

DREAMS AND NIGHTMARES

D eep sea blues across the swimming pool,

R unning through the heat.

E ach blade of grass unique in every way.

A magnificent stag patrolling its herd.

M eadows full of happiness,

S hade under the giant oak.

N obody moved.

I t was pitch black like a sky with no stars.

G iant rats scuttled across the floor,

H atred scarred their faces.

T he iron chains, so painful, so tight,

M y arm hung down, limp.

A n owl was heard in the distance.

R ose red blood dripped from my leg,

E ach breath could be my last,

S earching for light.

By Jacob Akrigg

Dream and Nightmare

Day starts then day finishes, I'm going to sleep so I can have a dream.

Really exciting things are about to happen as I fall into a deep sleep so that I can have a dream.

Everything is up to you and about you.

Anything you desire having you can have in your dream.

Many spectacular things are possible when you're in a dream.

AND

Non stop drama and emotion in your body as you're having a nightmare.

In a nightmare I dream (weird isn't it!) about not having the nightmare I have.

Gulp is the sound you'll make after you had a nightmare.

Haunted dreams and scary thoughts are all from one nightmare.

Thoughts creeping in your mind as you wish for it to be all over soon.

Many dreadful things occur to you when you're in a nightmare.

As you're in a nightmare your heart is pumping twice as fast.

Running away as your fear follows you.

Every fear you have all in one nightmare.

By Callum Bushell

Signed by our Authors and Illustrators
Reception

Year 1

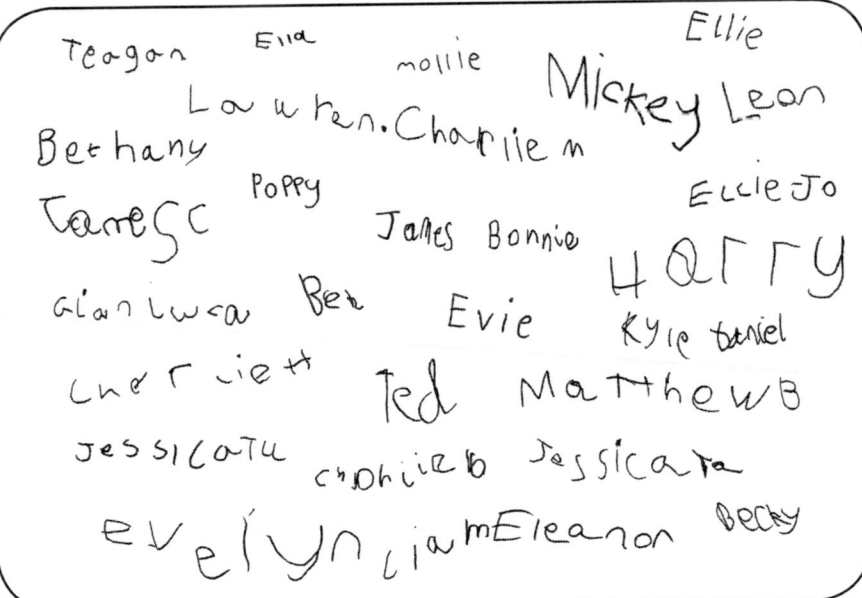

Year 2

Year 3

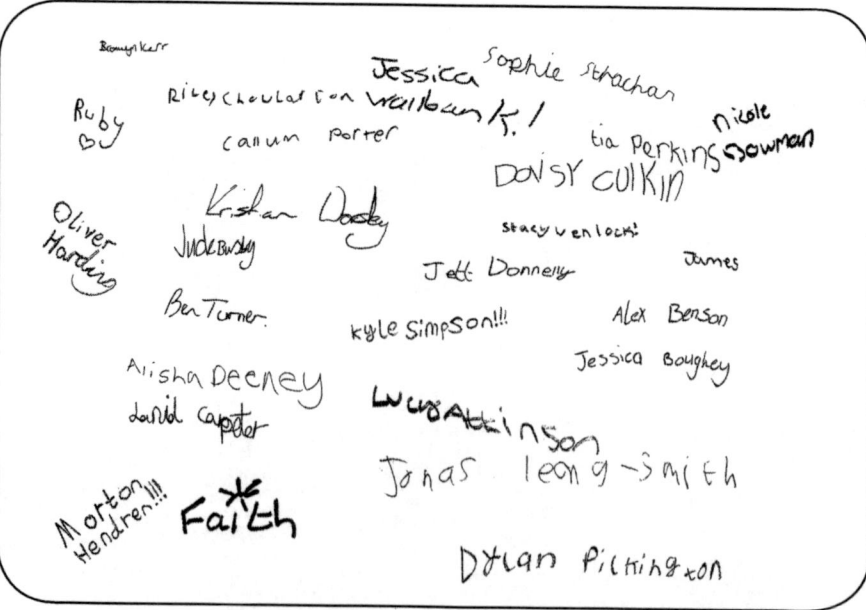

Year 4

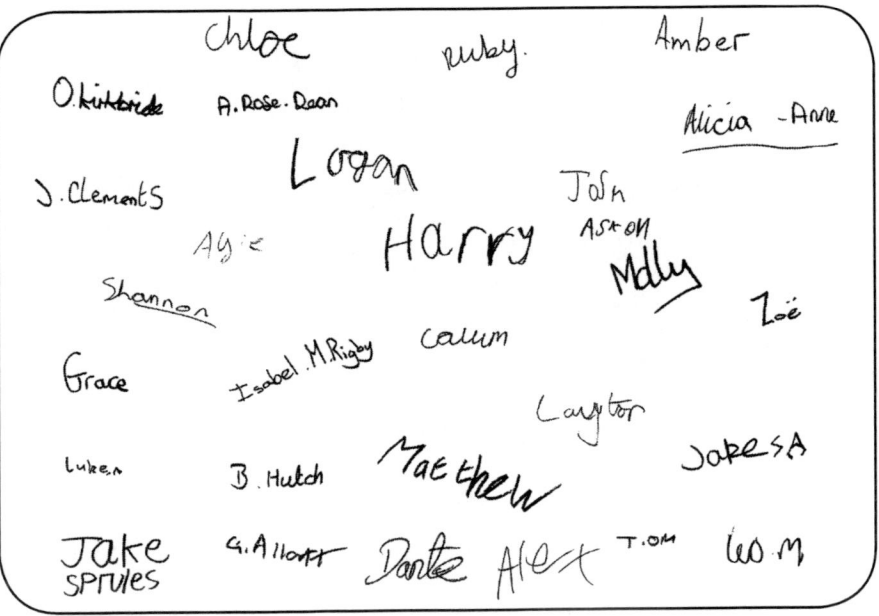

Year 5

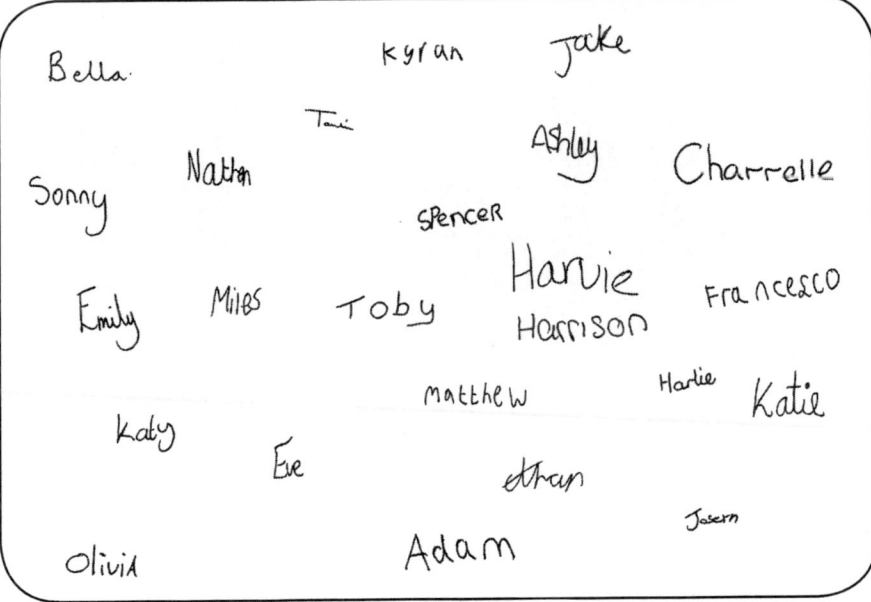

Year 6

Jacob A   Codie   Ruby   Seated   Tia.   callum
Maia   Megan Routh   Abbey
Samantha   Kayleigh   Erie Brook ☺
Jack   Chloe   Thomas B
Holly christie-Harrison
Lucy   Megan   Thomas R
Joe   Josh
Luke   Corban
Sophie   Rosanna Main

The
End